PERANAKAN CHINESE POLITICS IN INDONESIA

MARY F. SOMERS

PERANAKAN CHINESE POLITICS IN INDONESIA

EQUINOX
PUBLISHING
JAKARTA KUALA LUMPUR

EQUINOX PUBLISHING (ASIA) PTE LTD
No 3. Shenton Way
#10-05 Shenton House
Singapore 068805

www.EquinoxPublishing.com

Peranakan Chinese Politics In Indonesia
by Mary F. Somers

ISBN 978-602-8397-35-3

First Equinox Edition 2009

Printed in the United States

Cornell Modern Indonesian Project Interim Reports
This title was originally published as an "Interim Report" in the Cornell Modern Indonesia
Project (CMIP) series organized by the Cornell Southeast Asia Program. CMIP's first
"Interim Report" appeared in 1956, during an era when little scholarship on Indonesia
was available, and those studies that did appear often lagged far behind the actual events
taking place in the country. George Kahin, director of CMIP at the time, explained in
his foreword to the first "Interim Report" that these books were intended to address this
lack of timely scholarship and encourage lively critical exchanges among researchers and
readers. Therefore, as he explained, the "Interim Reports" would be "explicitly tentative and
provisional in character." We believe that an understanding of this historical context is key to
a full appreciation of these contributions to the study of Indonesia in the twentieth century.

TABLE OF CONTENTS

PREFACE

This report is the latest of the studies of the Chinese minority in Indonesia to be published by the Cornell Modern Indonesia Project. The Project has a long-term interest in this subject, and earlier studies which it has published include Giok-Lan Tan's *The Chinese of Sukabumi* and Donald E. Willmott's *The National Status of the Chinese in Indonesia 1900-1958*.

In the present Interim Report Mary F. Somers undertakes to view the overseas Chinese question as part of the politics of Indonesia, concentrating on the persons of Chinese descent who are Indonesian citizens. She devotes particular attention to the *peranakan* Chinese organization, Baperkip and the role it has played, both in Indonesia's Chinese community and generally on the Indonesian political scene. She is also concerned with the reaction of the *peranakan* Chinese to the possibility of cultural assimilation into Indonesian society and the willingness of the Indonesians to accept them.

After gaining her B. A. in History and Chinese Language at Trinity College in Washington, D. C., Miss Somers entered Cornell University in 1958 as a Ph. D. candidate in the Department of Government and Southeast Asia Program. Following an initial period of research at Cornell and an intensive study of the Chinese (Mandarin) and Indonesian languages, she carried out research in Indonesia from December 1961 to May 1963 under a Foreign Area Training Fellowship. While there she interviewed prominent Chinese widely — both in Java and in Sumatra (Palembang, Medan, Padang), in Sulawesi (Makassar) and in Kalimantan (Bandjarmasin, Pontianak, Singkawang).

Miss Somers wishes to emphasize that the conclusions she has reached in the report are tentative; and she hopes to develop them further in a forthcoming publication. She would, therefore, welcome any comments on or criticisms of her study.

Ithaca, N.Y.   George McT. Kahin
March 16, 1964   Director

ACKNOWLEDGMENTS

So many individuals in Indonesia assisted me in this research that it would be ungrateful to name only a few; therefore, let me say a collective thank you to them all. Particular thanks are due to Professor George McT. Kahin, Professor G. William Skinner, J. A. C. Mackie, and Daniel S. Lev for their comments on the draft of this report. Responsibility for any errors is, however, mine.

Cornell University   Mary F. Somers
Ithaca, New York
April 15, 1964

INTRODUCTION

This paper describes the way in which changes in Indonesian politics since the revolution have affected the Chinese in Indonesia, in particular, the so-called *peranakans*. It devotes attention to the development of Baperki, a *peranakan* community organization, and to the question of the citizenship of the Indonesian Chinese, In the period since 1960, a number of young *peranakans* have been systematically propagating the idea of assimilation; this paper also attempts to evaluate the prospects for assimilation against the background of both Indonesian and Chinese attitudes.

Historical patterns of Chinese settlement

Chinese had been coming to Indonesia long before the Europeans arrived in the archipelago. In fact, when the first Europeans arrived, there were already Chinese trading establishments in some of Java's ports, Despite centuries of residence in the islands, however, the Chinese rarely became part of the Indonesian community.

For one thing, contact between the two ethnic groups, apart from business transactions, was limited. Originally the resident Chinese community lived in a section of the port city close to the harbor. Their situation was similar to that of alien traders residing in other Asian cities: the Europeans in Canton before 1839 were confined to a special quarter, as were the Dutch in their earliest stay in Bantam. The remains of this pattern of settlement still persist in Java, and for the period from 1835 to 1919 the Dutch colonial government restricted the Chinese to residence in special quarters (*wijken*) of the major towns in Java.[1] Within these charters, special Chinese officers acted as agents of the Dutch government, Thus government of the Chinese population was managed by other Chinese; only at the higher levels did Chinese officers deal with the Dutch regime.[2] The colonial authority was, therefore, far removed from the average Chinese resident, and leaders of the Chinese community acted as go-betweens.

Alongside the quarter system a secondary pattern of settlement developed in Java, As the demand for agricultural products for export increased under colonial rule, both Chinese and Dutch profited from a kind of symbiosis, Chinese collected primary products from native growers and sold them to Dutch export firms. Imported finished goods traveled the reverse path, from Dutch importer through Chinese distributor to native consumer. This pattern was well-developed in Java under the East India Company's rule.[3]

In order to collect native products the Chinese needed to travel extensively and even to reside in the interior of Java. Residence limitations had thus to be relaxed, or even ignored. In 1920, only one year after the restrictions on Chinese residence had been formally repealed, about 58 per cent of the Chinese in West Java, 44 per cent of those in Central Java, and 34 per cent of those in East Java lived outside the 78 major cities and towns.[4]

Even when the Chinese lived in small towns and rural areas, they seldom developed a common life with the people of the area. This was partly a result of ethnic and religious differences, partly because of the greater mobility of the Chinese traders, whose business and family ties were in other towns, and partly because so many of the Chinese involved

---

1 Wouter Brokx, *Het recht tot wonen en tot reizen in Nederlandsch-Indië*'s Hertogenbosch: C.N. Teulings' Koninklijke Drukkerijen, 1925), pp. 29 and 183, Brokx points out that long before these restrictions came into effect, Chinese did live in separate sections of the cities.

2 See, for example, Liem Thian Joe, *Riwajat Semarang 1416-1931* (Semarang: Boekhandel Ho Kim Joe, c. 1933), pp. 9-10, on duties of the first Chinese officer in Semarang, who was appointed in 1672.

3 Liem Twan Djie, *De distribueerende tusschenhandel der Chineezen op Java* ('s-Gravenhage: Martinus Nijhoff, 1947), p. 27 and *passim*. Liem argues that this trade declined after 1929 as a result of the depression, Japanese competition and the growth of Indonesian cooperatives. It persisted nevertheless in the 1950's.

4 Adapted from *Volkstelling 1930*, Volume VII, *Chineezen en andere Vreemde Oosterlingen in Nederlandsch -Indië* (Batavia: Department van Economische Zaken, 1935), Tables 1 and 2.

in this intermediate trade (particularly in East Java in the interwar period) were recent immigrants.[5]

The third settlement pattern of the Chinese was, for Java, exceptional. A number of farmers of Chinese descent lived in the environs of Djakarta, and in a few other enclaves of the island. In the 17th century, a number of Chinese had already taken up sugar-growing in the Djakarta area, More important, under the private lands (*particuliere landerijen*) schemes of Governors Daendals and Raffles, considerable tracts of previously uncultivated land had been sold to Europeans and Chinese. Although the sales of such private lands were stopped in 1854 (and in practice ceased even earlier), and a regulation of 1875 expressly forbade the sale of agricultural land by Indonesian natives to non-natives, these tracts still remained in private hands.

Ownership of private lands included rights to levy taxes (in money, kind, or labor) from the population, and ownership was held in perpetuity. The people who lived on these lands were, in some cases, exploited and abused. Although by 1940 the colonial government had repurchased some 720,000 hectares (one hectare = 2.5 acres), over 400,000 hectares remained in private hands at that time. All but a few thousand hectares of the private lands were located in the three West Java residencies of Batavia (Djakarta), Buitenzorg (Bogor), and Krawang.[6] These land titles were ultimately abolished only after the Indonesian revolution.

Much of the land around Djakarta has been held in this kind of fief, particularly in the Tanggerang area to the west of the city. When the colonial government repurchased some of these lands, they were sold in smaller parcels to persons who had lived or worked on the original private estates, many of them Chinese. Thus, in this third instance, the

---

5   *Ibid.*, Table 14, shows that 20,000 of 28,000 foreign-born men listing an occupation in East Java were in trade; 48,000 of 74,000 in all Java. We cannot directly determine how many of these were in rural areas, but we do know that East Java had 44,000 alien Chinese in rural areas in 1957, compared to 15,000 for West Java and 12,000 for Central Java, according to the figures of Biro Pusat Statistik, *Penduduk Indonesia 1957* (Djakarta: 1959). These totals were obtained by subtracting the number of alien Chinese resident in capitals of first- and second-level autonomous areas from the total alien Chinese population. See also below, p. 26.

6   *Indisch Verslag 1941*, Part II, *Statistisch jaaroverzicht van Neder-landsch-Indië over het jaar 1940*, Tables 177 and 177A. In 1930, when the private lands were about 500,000 hectares in extent, over 1, 100,000 natives and 35,000 Chinese lived on those lands. All but 38,000 natives and about 700 Chinese lived on the lands in West Java. *Ibid.*, Table 8D.

position of the Chinese most nearly approached that of the Indonesians around them: they were farmers or field workers in a farming community. However, this pattern was true for only a small number of the Chinese in Java: only 5. 9 per cent of the total employed Chinese population of Java and Madura earned a living from "ordinary native agriculture" in 1930.[7]

Two other patterns of Chinese settlement deserve mention. In West Kalimantan, Chinese established themselves quite independently of Western penetration. Although trade had been carried on between that island and China for over 1000 years, it was only in the 18th century that Chinese migrated in force to its western part. They operated gold mines in the area north of Pontianak, and a number of Hakka Chinese took up farming in the area as well. Other Chinese traded in primary products from the interior, bringing them to the coast for processing and export, an economic arrangement which persists to this day. Throughout the 19th and early 20th centuries (and even up to the first half of 1963), the commercial ties of West Kalimantan were with Singapore and not Djakarta.[8]

In contrast, in East Sumatra and the islands of Bangka and Belitung many Chinese settled directly as a result of Western expansion. Chinese coolie labor was imported to work the European tobacco plantations in Deli (east coast of Sumatra) and the tin mines of Bangka and Belitung. Coolie immigration to the area fell sharply in the 1930's, and many of the immigrants returned to China; many remained, however, some of them shifting to farming. By 1930, 30,000 Chinese in Sumatra earned their living in farming.[9] In most of Sumatra, but in particular on the west coast, Chinese never developed as strong a position in intermediary trade as they held in Java or West Kalimantan, for enterprising Sumatrans pre-empted that role.[10]

---

7   *Volkstelling* 1930, Volume VII, Subsidiary Table 26.

8   See W. J. Cator, *The Economic Position of the Chinese in the Netherlands Indies* (Oxford: Blackwell, 1936), pp. 138-180.

9   *Volkstelling 1930*, Volume VII, Table 14. "Farming" here means either ordinary subsistence agriculture or market gardening.

10 See Cator, *op. cit.*, pp. 180-211 and 225-237 for a discussion of Chinese economic activity in Belitung, Bangka, and East Sumatra.

Peranakan-totok divisions

The Chinese of Indonesia are by no means a culturally homogeneous group, but divided into *totok* (literally, pure) and *peranakan* (local-born or even "mixed blood") elements. This *peranakan-totok* distinction affects Chinese activities and attitudes in Java so deeply that the two segments of the Chinese population can hardly be called a single community.

Despite the general separateness of Chinese and Indonesians, a large number of Chinese, particularly in Java, became adapted to many elements of the majority Indonesian culture. These were the *peranakans*, products of intermarriage between Chinese male immigrants and Indonesian women; their descendants, by virtue of their recognizably Chinese names, continued to be considered Chinese. Because of their relative isolation from China, descendants of these mixed marriages were frequently unable to speak Chinese; their mother tongue was Malay or an Indonesian language. As late as the 19th century "Chinese" society in Java was a *peranakan* society. Although *peranakan* Chinese culture resembled the Indonesian in language, style of dress and other manners, conversion of Chinese to Islam (at least after the coming of the Europeans) occurred only in exceptional circumstances, most often outside of Java in places where only a few Chinese lived among a strongly Moslem population. Children of the rare marriages between Chinese women and Indonesian men were completely assimilated as Indonesians.

At the end of the 19th century, Chinese immigration to Indonesia increased greatly. Chinese women began to arrive in force for the first time, and Chinese-Indonesian intermarriage consequently declined. These *totok*, or pure, Chinese probably stimulated increased interest in the motherland among the *peranakan* group as well. Children of the new immigrants, by virtue of their numbers and their greater contact with China,usually did not become *peranakans* as had their predecessors, but remained culturally *totok* Chinese.[11]

While this description is an oversimplification, it does point to a basic division in the Chinese community on Java. *Peranakan* Chinese

11 G. William Skinner is at work on a study of this crucial period in the history of the Chinese community of Java. See also his "The Chinese Minority," in Ruth T. McVey, ed. *Indonesia* (New Haven, Human Relations Area Files, 1963), pp. 97-117.

do not exist in this same sense elsewhere in Indonesia, although there are a number of Chinese communities with a settled, partly acculturated element outside of Java, for example, in Padang (West Sumatra), Makassar (Sulawesi) and parts of Bangka and West Kalimantan.

Peranakan organizations in Indies public life: broker politics

After 1900, as a result of the activities of both K'ang Yu-wei and Sun Yat-sen, the *totok* group became more involved in the politics of the Chinese mainland, either directly, through activities of the Kuomintang, or indirectly, through the influence of the Chinese schools. The *peranakans*, however, were discouraged from sending their children to Chinese schools by the opening of Dutch-language schools especially for Chinese.[12] The Dutch government was consciously trying to woo the Chinese away from the influence of the mainland, and in this it succeeded with the *peranakans*, but not with the *totok* group. In 1920, 13,000 Foreign Asiatic (90 per cent or more of these "Foreign Asiatics" would be Chinese; the rest, Arabs, Indians, or peninsula -born Malays) children were in Dutch-language elementary schools, compared to at least 14,000 in Chinese-language schools. In 1930-31, 25,000 Foreign Asiatics attended Dutch-language elementary schools and an estimated 30,000 Chinese children attended all Chinese-language schools.[13] The success of the Dutch-language schools partly accounts for the fact that the *peranakan* Chinese as a whole were, and are, basically uninterested in political activities, whether in China or in Indonesia.

Only a small number of *peranakans* were politically active in the interwar period. (The *totok* group offered support for the Kuomintang.) Their most influential political organization, the Chung Hua Hui (Chinese association), combined cooperation with the Dutch government in defense of *peranakan* economic and social interests with cultural loyalty to China. Any Chinese aid to Indonesian nationalists in the prewar

---

12 See Lea E. Williams, *Overseas Chinese Nationalism* (Glencoe, Ill.: The Free Press, 1960) for a fuller treatment of these movements, See also review article by G. William Skinner, "Java's Chinese Minority: Continuity and Change," *The Journal of Asian Studies*, May 1961, pp. 353-362.

13 1920 figures from Centraal Kantoor voor de Statistiek, *Statistisch jaaroverzicht van Nederlandsch-Indië 1926* (Weltevreden: Lands-drukkerij, 1927), Table 43, and for 1931 from *Indisch Verslag 1932*, Part II, Table 57 and *Volkstelling 1930*, Volume VII, p. 109.

period was most often motivated by sympathy for Asian nationalism and by anti-Dutch or anti-imperialist sentiment, but only very rarely by any identification with the fate of Indonesia or Indonesians. The best example of this attitude is provided by the editor of the daily *Sin Po*. In 1928 his was the first newspaper to publish the Indonesian anthem, "Indonesia Raja." Yet this editor encouraged his fellow *peranakans* to learn Chinese, and, although he had been born in Indonesia and educated in Dutch schools, he visited China a number of times, and considered himself a Chinese subject.[14]

There was a small movement of Chinese *peranakans*, particularly in Surabaja and Semarang, which did identify with the Indonesian nationalist movement. However, the PTI (*Partai Tionghoa Indonesia* — Indonesian Chinese Party), founded in 1932 in Surabaja, remained small. Its leaders tended to support Chinese cultural autonomy in the future Indonesian state, although some did foresee complete assimilation of the Chinese. The PTI belonged to the more conservative "cooperative" wing of the Indonesian nationalist movement; a PTI representative sat in the *Volksraad*.[15] Because it was not allied to the "non-cooperative" nationalist activities (such as those led by Soekarno or Hatta) which, in retrospect, seem to have been the mainstream of the movement, the PTI is not well known among Indonesian political leaders today, many of whom hold the view that all the *peranakan* Chinese were either pro-Dutch or indifferent to the cause of Indonesian independence.

In the immediate prewar period, the *peranakan* Chinese community in general favored minimal contact with the government. As under the

---

14 The composer of "Indonesia Raja," W. R. Soepratman, worked as a reporter for *Sin Po's* Malay-language edition, of which Kwee Kek Beng was the editor. Kwee Kek Beng, *Doea poeloe lima tahon sebagi wartawan* (Batavia: Kuo, 1948), pp. 35-3l. The song appeared in the weekly edition, November 10, 1928.

15 The *Volksraad* (People's Council) was established in 1917 as a purely advisory body, but in 1927 it was given "co-legislative" powers with the Governor-General of the Indies. Many Indonesian nationalists refused to cooperate with the *Volksraad* (hence the name "non-cooperative," as opposed to the "cooperative" nationalists). At the time that a PTI member sat in the *Volksraad* (1935-39), 30 of its 60 members were Indonesians, 25 Europeans, 4 Chinese and 1 Arab. Of the Indonesian members, however, 11 were appointed by the government, as were 10 Europeans, 1 Chinese and 1 Arab. Even the elected members were chosen from a limited electorate (10 per cent of the Indonesians were eligible to vote) by an indirect system. See George McT. Kahin, *Nationalism and Revolution in Indonesia* (Ithaca, N. Y.: Cornell University Press, 1952), pp. 39-41.

old Chinese officers (whose positions had been gradually abolished by the 1930's), *peranakan* organizations continued to act as brokers for the community in its dealings with officials. Some organizations upheld Chinese economic interests. Schools attracted considerable attention, although control of the Chinese - language schools came increasingly within the province of the *totoks*. A multitude of Chinese youth, music, sport, and social organizations existed, not to mention the religious associations. These were often divided along *peranakan-totok* lines. Political activity as such, whether directed toward Chinese or Indonesian affairs, attracted only a tiny minority of all Chinese.

Ten years later, at the end of the Indonesian revolution there was no great change in the situation for the majority of *peranakans*, although the establishment of the People's Republic of China induced even the *peranakan* group to take a greater interest in mainland Chinese affairs. Their lack of interest in Indonesian politics stood in sharp contrast to the growing political consciousness of Indonesians in both towns and villages.

CHAPTER ONE
BAPERKI

Any discussion of the Chinese peranakan community in Indonesia in the past decade must revolve around the development of Baperki (Badan Permusjawaratan Kewarganegaraan Indonesia — Consultative Body for Indonesian Citizenship). This body was founded in March 1954, when the need for a new political organization for the Indonesian Chinese was all too apparent, and it now monopolizes the defense of the interests of those peranakan Chinese who are Indonesian citizens.

Previous Chinese political activity

Prior to 1954, a number of Chinese *peranakans* had joined Indonesian political parties. Liem Koen Hian (founder of the PTI), Oei Tjong Hauw, Oey Tiang Tjoei and Tan Eng Hoa served in the Committee for the Investigation of Indonesian Independence during the Japanese Occupation.[1] Tan Ling Djie was in the leadership of the PKI (*Partai Komunis Indonesia* — Indonesian Communist Party) from 1949 to 1953. Tan Po Goan had risen to cabinet rank during the Indonesian revolution and continued to serve in the PSI (*Partai Sosialis Indonesia* — Indonesian Socialist Party). In the cabinet in power at the time of Baperki's establishment, Chinese held portfolios of Health (Dr. Lie Kiat Teng, PSII — *Partai Sarekat Islam Indonesia*) and Finance (One Eng Die, PNI, *Partai Nasional Indonesia*). In fact, virtually all parties welcomed members of Chinese descent if they were at the same time financial supporters.

---

1 Benedict R. O'G. Anderson, *Some Aspects of Indonesian Politics under the Japanese Occupation: 1944-1945* (Ithaca, N. Y.: Cornell Modern Indonesia Project, 1961), p. 18.

In addition, there existed a weak "Chinese-Indonesian Democratic Party" (PDTI). This party was not only weak in membership, having by its own estimate only 27 branches in 1951;[2] but it was also weak in political influence. Its chairman, Thio Thiam Tjong, was tainted by his cooperation with the Dutch. During the colonial period he had been a leader of the Chung Hua Hui, an organization considered by Indonesians to have been in opposition to Indonesian nationalism. Even more damaging, however, was Thio's service of the Dutch government during the Indonesian revolution: he had acted as adviser for Chinese Affairs to Lieutenant Governor-General Van Mook. Given the political situation in Indonesia subsequent to 1950, one in which participation in the revolution was a criterion of fitness for leadership, Thio's background was not only damaging to him personally: his record of cooperation with the Dutch also prevented him from playing an influential role in Indonesian politics on behalf of the Chinese community.

Problem of discrimination

By early 1954 the economic policies of the Indonesian government were in serious conflict with Chinese business interests, and neither the PDTI nor the Chinese *peranakans* who had joined Indonesian parties seemed able to alleviate the situation. Successive cabinets in Indonesia from 1950 on had tried to restrict the role of foreign enterprise in the Indonesian economy, a policy which affected both large-scale Dutch enterprises and small, Chinese-owned shops. As most of the rules and regulations distinguished between "citizens" and "aliens," it soon became obvious to the Chinese that for a person who wished to continue doing business in Indonesia it would be advantageous to be an Indonesian citizen.

Since 1950, however, in addition to discriminating between citizens and non-citizens, Indonesian cabinets had reserved special privileges for the economic activities of indigenous (*asli*) Indonesians, as against citizens of foreign (i, e., Chinese) descent. This was particularly true in the field

---

2   Kementerian Penerangan Republik Indonesia, *Kepartaian di Indonesia* (Djakarta: Pepora 8, rev. ed., 1951), pp. 366-373.

of importing, where relatively quick. Sure, and substantial profits could be gained. The ostensible purpose of this discrimination was to foster the development of an indigenous business class; in practice it benefitted the supporters of the political parties controlling the government. Not infrequently, an indigenous Indonesian turned his import privileges to quick profit, either by selling them to a Chinese businessman outright or by forming a partnership in which the Chinese supplied the capital and the Indonesian, the political influence. Policies favoring *asli* businessmen became more strict during the first Ali Sastroamidjojo (PNI) cabinet (July 1953-July 1955), and the Chinese were beginning to feel the pressure of them.[3]

Citizenship

The fact that the citizenship of the Chinese, even the *peranakans*, was still unsettled also provided an occasion for *asli*-preference policies. The laws which determined Indonesian citizenship had left those Chinese who qualified for citizenship with no documentary proof of their status.[4]

Yet Chinese names are readily distinguished from Indonesian names, and the Indonesian government employees frequently assume that a person with a Chinese name is an alien unless he can prove otherwise. In order to obtain the necessary permits to do business, Chinese claiming to be Indonesian citizens were frequently asked to prove their citizenship, which, in 1954, they could not do. Since perhaps half of the Chinese in Indonesia were aliens, and there was no simple way of distinguishing them from the Chinese who were Indonesian citizens, the government was not completely unjustified in its requirements.

Indonesians viewed Chinese citizenship as a problem, not only because so much of the economy was in "alien" hands, but also because

---

3 See Nan Grindle Amstutz, *Development of Indigenous Importers in Indonesia, 1950-1955* (Dissertation: Fletcher School of Law and Diplomacy, May 1958).

4 Both the 1946 law on citizenship and the Round Table Agreement between Indonesia and the Netherlands on December 27, 1949, stipulated that persons of Chinese descent born in Indonesia of resident parents should make a court declaration within a specified time if they wished to reject Indonesian citizenship. Those who took no action within that time (two years, in the case of the Round Table Agreement) were considered to be Indonesian citizens. To prove that he had not rejected Indonesian citizenship, a Chinese born in Indonesia would have to request a search of the court records for the times of the choice periods, a cumbersome and unsatisfactory procedure.

of the role of the citizenship question in international relations. Since at least 1909, successive governments of China had claimed the loyalty of all Chinese living abroad. The 1929 citizenship law of Nationalist China, for example, recognized as Chinese citizens all children of Chinese fathers, wherever their birth. The law made no provision for rejection or loss of Chinese citizenship through acquisition of another nationality except with permission of China 's Ministry of Interior. In practice (and despite a consular convention to the contrary signed in 1911), representatives of the Chinese government treated all Chinese in Indonesia as citizens of China.[5]

In 1954, the Indonesian government determined to settle the citizenship question for the Chinese in Indonesia. The cabinet was then proposing a law which would greatly restrict the citizenship of persons of alien descent. Discussions were also under way with the People's Republic of China to limit, through an international agreement, her claims on citizenship of Indonesia's Chinese,

Because these citizenship laws would touch on their interests, especially in the economic field, the Chinese themselves felt the need of an organization to defend them. The PDTI could not handle the task, and in February 1954 it determined to dissolve itself.[6] Nor did the Indonesian political parties provide a satisfactory alternative; parties which otherwise might seem attractive to Chinese (such as the PNI) were themselves initiating objectionable measures on economic and citizenship questions.

Still another factor contributed to the need for a new and separate Chinese political organization at that time. Under the Indonesian Constitution, a number of seats in Parliament were reserved for members or representatives from the Chinese, European, and Arab minorities. It was argued that the only way to insure proper representation of Chinese interests in Parliament would be to found an organization which could compete for these seats in the general elections scheduled for 1955.[7]

---

5 For a more complete treatment of the citizenship question, see Donald E. Willmott, *The National Status of the Chinese in Indonesia, 1900-1958* (Ithaca, N. Y.: Cornell Modern Indonesia Project, 1961). 1929 citizenship law cited in Liem Tjeng Hien-Kho, *Perdjandjian Dwikewarganegaraan R. I. -R. R. T. dan pelaksanaannja* (Djakarta: Keng Po, I960), pp. 243-247.

6 *Star Weekly*, 27 February 1954.

7 *Ibid.*, 20 March 1954. A symbol of the new organization, the lotus, was chosen at its first meeting,

Baperki established to defend Chinese

Those who took the initiative in forming the new organization were young, western-educated *peranakan* Chinese. In fact, the inauguration of Baperki took place in the building of the Sin Ming Hui, Djakarta's leading *peranakan* social organization. The name Baperki (*Badan Permusjawara-tan Kewarganegaraan Indonesia* — Consultative Body for Indonesian Citizenship) was in itself significant: the word "Chinese" was dropped from the title, and membership was open to all Indonesian citizens. On the other hand, *only* citizens were admitted, so that an alien Chinese could not join the organization. (The PDTI membership had been limited to Indonesian citizens in 1950.) Also interesting is the use of "*musjawarat*" (*permus-jawaratan* — consultative) in the title, because this is a popular word in contemporary Indonesian politics, referring to a way of arriving at a decision by consensus and not by debate and division. Thus the new organization expressed its devotion to peculiarly Indonesian political processes.

The group chose as chairman a *peranakan*, Siauw Giok Tjhan, who had been associated with the Indonesian government during the revolution. He had been in the PTI before the war, but had not been active in *peranakan* politics after 1950, although he was a member of the provisional Parliament, Siauw was the first editor of the newspaper of the PKI, *Harian Rakjat*, from 1951 to the end of 1953. Although most officers of the new organization had previously been prominent in the old PDTI (Thio Thiam Tjong, for example, was retained as one of the vice-chairmen), the vigorous leadership of Siauw contributed significantly to the growth of Baperki's political power in subsequent years.

The elections of 1955

Although consistently referring to itself as a "mass organization," Baperki behaved very much like a political party in the first years of its existence. Thus, it put up candidates in the 1955 national and 1957 regional

for use on the election ballot, even though the group was not supposed to represent any particular political viewpoint. *Star Weekly* itself had not wanted the new group to put up candidates under its own name. (27 February 1954)

elections. Its symbol, the lotus, was the first choice of the majority of Chinese voters in Java. Although a few Indonesians joined its leadership, and eventually it also recruited some members from the Arab and Indian minority communities, both Indonesian and Chinese considered Baperki to be the Chinese party, and the Chinese voters supported it accordingly. It gained 178, 887 votes in the 1955 Parliamentary elections and 160,456 in the elections for the Constituent Assembly from a potential electorate of perhaps 500,000 citizen Chinese.

The following table is a breakdown of the Baperki vote in 1955, by provinces.[8]

Baperki Vote in 1955 Elections
by province

	Parliament	*Constituent Assembly*
East Java	35,489	33,369
Central Java	44,743	43,908
West Java	38,376	33,595
Djakarta	26,944	23,384
South Sumatra	10,178	8,496
Central Sumatra	4,495	*
North Sumatra	4,674	4,044
South Kalimantan	2,152	1,981
East Kalimantan	536	441
North Sulawesi	2,195	2,100
South Sulawesi	1,462	1, 164
East Nusatenggara	3,784	1,111
West Nusatenggara	3,859	1,981

*not listed

---

8 Provincial figures in a communication from A. van Marie. See also his "The First Indonesian Parliamentary Elections," *Indonesië*, 1956, No, 3, pp. 257-264. Totals according to Herbert Feith, *The Indonesian Elections of 1955* (Ithaca, N. Y.: Cornell Modern Indonesia Project, 1957), pp. 65-72. Panitya Pemilihan Indonesia, *Indonesia memilih* (Djakarta, 1958), p. 147.

Baperki did not enter the elections in West Kalimantan or Maluku. It made no vote-pooling arrangements with other parties in either election.

Siauw's role in Parliament: minority representation

Siauw's personality was as important an influence in parliamentary politics as the size and strength of the organization he represented. He was a member of the section on economics of Parliament, the Parliamentary Consultative Committee, and the credentials committee of the Constituent Assembly. He helped organize the National Progressive fraction, a coalition of radical left-wing parties which had only one or two representatives apiece. Siauw was able to persuade President Soekarno to receive or address Baperki delegations. He was a member of the 1956 parliamentary delegation to the People's Republic of China and the 1957 parliamentary delegation to the USA.

The way Siauw handled the battle for the seats allotted to minority-representatives is one indication of his influence. The 1950 Provisional Constitution of Indonesia and the election laws stipulated that the three ethnic minorities in Indonesia should be guaranteed representation in Parliament: nine members for those of Chinese descent, six for those of European descent, and three for those of Arab descent.[9]

---

9 Seats in the Indonesian Parliament and Constituent Assembly were filled by proportional representation. In 1955, Baperki, with nearly 180,000 votes, obtained one seat on the first apportionment and had a surplus (*sisa suara*) of about 30,000 votes. Since the number of seats parceled out in the first apportionment would be less than that stipulated by the election law (because of the manner of division), additional seats were awarded to the various parties on the basis of the size of their surplus. In this second apportionment, vote-pooling arrangements came into play; two or more parties could agree to pool their leftover votes in order to obtain an additional seat jointly. (Such arrangements had to be announced before the elections because votes cast for one party might thus be given to the candidate of another party.) In the 1955 elections, Baperki made no vote-pooling agreements. (In the 1957 regional elections, however, Baperki made such arrangements with a number of other parties on a local basis; see below, pp. 18-19.) Next to the PKI, which in 1955 also made no vote-pooling agreements, Baperki had the largest surplus after the final apportionment of seats. Baperki was later to argue that its large surplus demonstrated its popularity and entitled it to special consideration in the allotment of seats for minority representatives.

After seats in Parliament had been assigned to the parties according to the above method, the election committee was to inform the cabinet of the number of persons from each of the ethnic minorities who had been elected to Parliament. If the number elected from any group was less than the guaranteed representation for that group, the government was required to appoint additional members in accordance with the wish of each group, increasing, if necessary, the total number of seats in Parliament. (The same provisions applied to the Constituent Assembly,

In 1955, more than three persons of Arab descent had been elected to Parliament from the party lists, as well as two Chinese: Siauw of Baperki and Tjoo Tik Tjoen of the PKI. This meant that seven more Chinese and six Europeans should be appointed to seats. As the two largest parties, the Masjumi and PNI, had equal numbers of seats in Parliament, the appointment of these thirteen minority representatives could be used to rearrange the power balance. This is just what happened, for the new cabinet at first announced a list of thirteen minority representatives, all but one of whom came from cabinet-supporting parties.

Baperki was not a cabinet-supporting party, and when the cabinet proposed to fill the minority seats without regard to its own proposed candidates (for whom a reported 23,000 persons had signed a petition), Baperki, led by Siauw, raised such a storm that the cabinet finally withdrew one of its appointees and replaced him with a Baperki man. The battle then shifted to the Constituent Assembly, which was elected according to the same system a few months later. There, candidates selected by Baperki were in the first three places of the thirteen appointments of Chinese.[10] This whole struggle, which ended only in November 1957, was an indication for the Chinese that *only* Baperki was really interested in and capable of defending them.

Dual citizenship treaty with China

Siauw also found a possible solution for the Chinese affected by the dual citizenship treaty. This treaty, signed in April 1955 by Indonesian Foreign Minister Soenario and Chinese Foreign Minister Chou En-lai, affected persons previously considered citizens of both China and Indonesia. About half of Indonesia's 2,300,000 Chinese residents fell into

---

except that the number of minority representatives was doubled.) To assure that the appointment would be in accordance with the wishes of the groups concerned, the election committee was directed to inform the government of the names of candidates from the minority groups who were unsuccessful and the votes received by each.

Provisions for minority representatives are contained in articles 58 and 135 of the Provisional Constitution, articles 99 and 136 of the Election Law (Law number 7 of 1953), and article 81 of Government Regulation Number 9 of 1954 on implementation of the Election Law. See R. S. Palindih, ed., *Undang-undang dan Peraturan-peraturan Pemilihan Umum* (Djakarta: Bulan Bintang, 1954).

10 This account is based on a number of Djakarta press accounts from 1956 and 1957.

this category.[11] According to the treaty, these persons might renounce their Chinese citizenship by filing a declaration choosing Indonesian citizenship within a two-year period after the exchange of instruments of ratification of the treaty. The status of the rest of Indonesia's Chinese, who were not considered to be Indonesian citizens, was unaffected by the treaty.[12]

This treaty met with considerable opposition from the *peranakan* Chinese community, however, for a Chinese who considered himself an Indonesian citizen was thereby forced to go through a potentially cumbersome procedure to verify his Indonesian citizenship, which he would otherwise lose. Indonesian insistence on this provision would make many Chinese aliens, and economic discrimination against these aliens would probably follow.

Voter exemption from the treaty

Actually, ratification of the dual citizenship treaty put both Baperki and the PKI in a dilemma. Both wanted to support any agreement with the People's Republic of China. In 1955, the PKI was a cabinet-supporting party, so it wished to support the cabinet's decisions, too. On the other hand, the provisions of the treaty were highly objectionable to the citizen Chinese of Indonesia, and both parties were anxious to defend Chinese interests. Because of the vigorous protests against the treaty, a set of notes exchanged between Prime Minister Ali Sastroamidjojo and Chou Enlai were appended to the treaty. These notes provided that Indonesia might exempt a number of its citizens of Chinese descent from rejecting Chinese citizenship, because their loyalty to Indonesia rather than China was already proved by their social and political position.[13]

From the beginning it was clear that persons who had served in the cabinet or Parliament or had represented Indonesia abroad would

---

11 They were Indonesian citizens by virtue of the Round Table Agreement which provided that Chinese born in Indonesia of resident parents (before December 27, 1949) would be considered Indonesian citizens unless they rejected Indonesian citizenship, in court, before December 27, 1951. They were at the same time Chinese citizens because of China's claim to all persons of Chinese descent. See also above, pp.9-10.

12 Willmott, *op. cit.*, pp. 47-48.

13 *Ibid.*, pp. 54-56.

be exempt from making a court declaration of choice of Indonesian citizenship. But this would affect only a few hundred people. Siauw suggested that all those who had voted in the elections be considered exempt from making a choice. Since 180,000 persons, virtually all of them Chinese, had voted for Baperki alone, this exemption of voters would have meant that a substantial proportion of the adult citizens of Chinese descent would have their citizenship rights assured with a minimum of red tape.

Although a Baperki official later estimated that 65 per cent of Indonesian citizens of Chinese descent were covered by the voter-exemption provision,[14] this was probably true only in Java. In 1955, Java had about 600,000 citizen Chinese,[15] of whom at least half would have been eligible to vote. Baperki obtained about 145,000 votes in Java that year; virtually all of these would have been from Chinese. Other Chinese who voted, but not for Baperki, might total at the highest 50,000. This would give a maximum of 195,000 adult Chinese citizens who participated in the 1955 elections, that is, nearly two-thirds of the adult citizen Chinese of Java at that time, and these would all be exempt from the requirement of renouncing Chinese citizenship.

Outside of Java, where Baperki itself gained only about 33,000 votes, and where citizen Chinese were apparently not so active in voting, the provision would have less meaning. Perhaps less than one-quarter of the adult citizen Chinese outside of Java would have benefitted from this voter-exemption provision.

Nevertheless, given the intention of the treaty, which was largely to reduce the number of citizen Chinese in Indonesia, the exemption of these several thousand persons from the requirement of declaring actively for Indonesian citizenship was significant.

By supporting the voter-exemption provision, the PKI and Baperki were able to escape from their dilemma. They could support the treaty as a whole, indicating a rapprochement with the People's Republic of China, and yet, by virtue of the voter-exemption clause, nullify its more objectionable effects. After the treaty was finally ratified by Parliament,

---

14 Interview 1962.
15 Based on figures collected for the election lists and published in *Penduduk Indonesia 1956* and *1957*.

in December 1957, the Indonesian government announced its refusal
to accept voters as being exempt from the choice. Some members of
Parliament seem to have agreed to the treaty with the understanding that
voters would be exempted, and, in fact, the treaty would probably not
have been ratified but for this mistaken understanding.[16]

Assaatism

Baperki also demonstrated its ability to defend Chinese interests by
taking up the fight against Assaatism.[17] This was a movement, especially
powerful in 1956-57, which proposed that the Indonesian government
adopt a policy favoring the economic interests of the *asli* (indigenous)
group, if necessary at the expense of citizens of alien (Chinese) descent.
The Assaat movement openly promoted a policy of discrimination against
citizen Chinese and urged that this discrimination be carried out more
explicitly and systematically than at any time previously.

Assaat and his followers blamed Dutch colonial policy for having made
the indigenous Indonesians "economically weak," leaving those of alien
descent "economically strong." No one doubted that the real purpose of
the proposal was to give special privileges to organizations of indigenous
Indonesian businessmen, for Assaat himself initially introduced his
ideas to a meeting of these businessmen. In fact, Assaat's speeches show
how racial these ideas were, for he proposed that the discrimination be
directed solely against the Chinese and not against citizens of Arab or
Dutch descent.[18] Had it been purely a matter of erasing colonial policy,
the Arab *peranakans* would logically have been included, since their legal
position in colonial society had been virtually the same as that of the

---

16 Willmott, *op. cit.*, pp. 56-61. Willmott points out that opposition to the treaty had been so great,
   even among parties which were then supporting the cabinet, that it was doubtful that it could
   have been ratified. Some members who opposed the treaty interpreted a statement of Foreign
   Minister Subandrio to mean that voters would be exempted in the implementation of the treaty
   and dropped their opposition, causing the treaty to be ratified unanimously in December. At the
   beginning of 1958 the cabinet denied that it had ever intended to exempt voters.

17 Assaat, a lawyer and leader of the Masjumi party, had been Acting President of Indonesia during
   the revolution (when Soekarno and Hatta were captured by the Dutch). At the onset of the
   movement which bore his name, he was chairman of an indigenous importers' association.

18 Assaat, "Perlindungan Chusus" reprinted in Badan Pekerdja Kensi Pusat, *Kensi berdjuang*
   (Djakarta: Djambatan, 1957), pp. 51-62.

Chinese, while the Dutch were most favored of all.

Baperki immediately reacted to the challenge, Assaat's keynote speech was given to an importers' congress in Surabaja held between March 19 and 23, 1956. On March 29, *Republik* published a statement of the Baperki central committee, expressing disappointment with Assaat's position because it was so clearly based on racial discrimination. Siauw, in another statement, denied that business practices of citizen Chinese were monopolistic or in any way detrimental to the Indonesian economy, as Assaat had charged.[19] When the Assaatists clamored for protection of the "economically weak" (Indonesian) businessman against the "economically strong" (Chinese), Baperki argued that protection of the economically weak was eminently desirable, but that the determination of just who *was* economically weak must be on a class basis and not according to race.[20]

That the PKI supported Baperki energetically on the issue of Assaatism is one evidence of the cooperation of the two groups. One of its Chinese members of Parliaments, Tjoo Tik Tjoen, called Assaatism nonsense and race discrimination.[21] Later, the party went even further, calling any enemy of the Chinese, the nationalists, or the PKI an enemy of the Indonesian revolution and urging unity against the threat of Dutch imperialism. The economic editor of the party's paper applied the epithet "*Soska*" (*sosialis kanan* — right-wing socialist) to Assaat and his followers.[22] That epithet is a significant one, for it was usually reserved for the PSI and Masjumi. The Masjumi, always an opponent of the PKI, had been the strongest supporter of Assaat. In this case, the PKI was opposing Assaat because it opposed the Masjumi, wishing to discredit it and, by association, the PSI, which was also an anti-PKI party. No doubt the PKI was also worried that its opponents had seized on a popular and potentially extremely powerful issue. Given the political situation in 1956, the PKI attitude was motivated as much by rivalry with Masjumi as by need or desire to defend the Chinese.

Although dual citizenship had been used previously as a pretext for

---

19 *Persbiro Indonesia* (PIA) dispatch, 29 March 1956. *Republik*, a Djakarta daily newspaper, although not officially associated with Baperki, served as mouthpiece for its central committee until it closed in 1960.
20 *Republik*, 23 June 1956.
21 *Republik*, 31 May 1956.
22 *Harian Rakjat*, 17 and 23 August 1956.

discrimination against the Chinese, Assaatism was the first such blatant attack on the citizen Chinese, and its challenge was not limited to the economic field. The discussion of the supposedly favored position of the Chinese caused some observers to fear outbreaks of communal violence. That the movement died quickly in 1958 was less a result of Baperki (and PKI) opposition than of the political changes taking place in Indonesia at the time, the rise of regional problems, and particularly Assaat's own defection to the regional rebellion in Sumatra.[23]

1957 elections

In 1957, Baperki mobilized its forces for participation in the regional elections, paying more attention to these elections than any major party except the PKI.[24] In the elections for regional assemblies in Central Java, West Java, Djakarta, and South Kalimantan, Baperki's votes in 1957 were almost the same as in the national election of 1955. Those of other parties, except the PKI, fell sharply. In South Sumatra, Bapkerki's votes increased slightly, from 10, 178 to 12, 816. In East Java, it made a spectacular gain, from 35,489 in 1955 to 70, 770 in 1957. Articles in *Republik* from this period indicate that Baperki was exerting greatest efforts in East Java, where Siauw Giok Tjhan's brother was provincial chairman. Assuming that relatively few non-Chinese voted for Baperki, then nearly every Chinese in East Java who voted must have voted for that organization, as East Java had a total citizen Chinese population of 155,398 in 1957.[25]

In 1957, Baperki decided to allow its local branches to sign votepooling agreements with other parties, but it left the choice of parties to local option. In the provincial election for East Java, in the city of Probolinggo,

---

23 G. William Skinner, "Overseas Chinese in Southeast Asia," *The Annals*, January 1959, p. 141.

24 Ruth T. McVey, "Indonesian Communism and the Transition to Guided Democracy," in A.D. Barnett, ed., *Communist Strategies in Asia* (New York: Praeger, 1963), esp. pp. 153 and 159, relates PKI gains in the 1957-58 regional elections to its strategy of cultivating mass support.

25 *Penduduk Indonesia 1957*. Just over half of these, that is about 85,000, would have been of voting age, but not all of these would have voted. East Java was still considered to be Baperki's best organized province in 1962, when the organization was helping with implementation of the dual citizenship treaty. The area's Chinese have a long tradition of political activity; in addition to giving birth to PTI and a number of *peranakan* leaders, East Java Chinese had a tradition of non-cooperation with the Dutch during the Indonesian revolution. Clearly, in 1957 Baperki received several thousand non-Chinese votes.

in the regencies of Malang, Ngandjuk, Probolinggo and Tulungagung (all East Java), and in the regencies of Grobogan and Purworedjo (Central Java), Baperki allied with the PKI. But especially in areas of PKI weakness, such as West Java and the islands outside Java, Baperki chose to ally itself with other parties. Its choice ranged from other members of the National Progressive fraction in Parliament, through the PNI, PSI, and the Christian parties, to IPKI (Upholders of Indonesian Independence, a small party whose main support was in West Java) and the Islamic PSII It had as many vote-pooling agreements with the Catholic Party as with the PKI (i.e., in seven places). The variety of parties with which local branches of Baperki allied themselves demonstrates the range of political attitudes held by these branches.[26]

Baperki representatives cooperated with the PKI in organizing the assemblies of Semarang, Salatiga, and Probolinggo, for example, but in the first two Baperki support was superfluous because the PKI already-held a majority of the seats in the assembly.[27]

Since 1957 Baperki's role has shifted more away from politics to community services such as the operation of schools and legal assistance services. Elections have not been held since 1957 and may not be held for some time. Even if they were in the offing, Baperki could not participate because it is not recognized as a political party under the terms of the decree for simplification of parties (Presidential Regulation No. 7 of 1959). Baperki leaders still sit in the regional assemblies, but as "non-party" people. Likewise, Siauw is a member of the appointed "Gotong-Rojong" Parliament, but since most of its discussions take place in camera, it no longer acts as a forum for his protests against discrimination.

Chinese schools question

Baperki still retains considerable influence on the Indonesian scene, however, Its alliance with Soekarno has served it well; so has its left-wing orientation and its cooperation with the PKI. Most important, its

---

26 All election statistics and data on vote-pooling arrangements from Kernenterian Dalam Negeri, Biro Pemilihan, *Daftar angka-angka hasil Pemilihan DPRD tahun 1957* (mimeographed, n. d.).

27 Accounts of the elections and the organization of the regional assemblies are contained in *Rejpublik, Keng Po, Sin Po, Harian Rakjat*, 1957.

increasing emphasis on community services has made it more influential among the Indonesian Chinese. One reason for its increasing influence among the Chinese stems from the attempt by the Indonesian government to reduce the influence of mainland Chinese culture and politics among Indonesian citizens of Chinese descent by attacks on alien Chinese schools, Baperki's response was to establish schools itself.

During the Japanese occupation a number of Chinese *peranakan* children entered Chinese-language schools because the Dutch-language schools had been closed. The Chinese schools continued to attract pupils after the war, although a few *peranakans* did enter their children in the resurrected Dutch schools and more began to send their children to Indonesian-language schools. A report in 1948 estimated that 85 per cent of all Chinese children in elementary schools in Dutch-controlled areas of Indonesia were in Chinese-language schools.[28] This was a much higher percentage than for the prewar period, and it meant that many *peranakan* children whose parents spoke only Dutch and/or Indonesian were being "re-sinified" by an education emphasizing Chinese language, culture, and politics.

The Indonesian government was doubly apprehensive about this trend. Not only were its citizens receiving an education geared to life in another country, but the political struggles between pro-Communist and Kuomintang Chinese, which centered on control of the schools, were becoming a threat to public order.[29] Furthermore, even some non-Chinese students were being attracted to the newer and better Chinese schools.

The government found it difficult to police the Chinese schools, primarily because there were few inspectors with a command of the Chinese language. In parts of West Kalimantan, for example, Chinese

---

28 *Star Weekly*, 5 March 1950. Since the Republic of Indonesia controlled less than two-thirds of Sumatra and about half of the island of Java (Bantam, Central Java excluding Semarang, and a small part of East Java) the Dutch-controlled territory referred to here would be the rest of present-day Indonesia. Because the Dutch at this time — controlled the major cities of Indonesia, except Jogjakarta, Solo, Madiun, Kediri, and Padang-Bukittinggi, their territory probably held over 80 per cent of the Chinese and Chinese schools. In 1955, Donald Willmott estimated that one-third of *peranakan* school children in Semarang were in Chinese schools. See *The Chinese of Semarang* (Ithaca, N. Y.: Cornell University Press, 1960), p. 175.

29 In 1951, for example, open fighting broke out between Communist and Kuomintang supporters in Palembang. Interview 1962.

schools had sprung up in out-of-the-way villages, and the Department of Education could not even be certain how many foreign-language medium schools existed in Indonesia, much less subject them to inspection and control.[30]

Despite the efforts of the Department to deal with this situation between 1950 and 1957, by requiring the schools to register and by insisting that school directors demonstrate their ability to speak Indonesian, it was the military who precipitated a crisis. Acting under the authority of the state of emergency (*keadaan darurat perang*) of March 1957, the Military Governor of Nusatenggara closed all Chinese alien schools in that area on May 31, 1957.[31] His policy spread to other areas in the following months. The attacks on the Chinese schools developed into an attack on the Chinese in general, part of the campaign against the Kuomintang, and, at the same time, an attempt to reduce the influence of all foreign education in Indonesia.

Six months later, in November 1957, the Djakarta military headquarters eased the terms of the prohibition of alien schools, but extended them to the nation as a whole. Six more months were allowed for implementation. All Indonesian citizens were forbidden to attend "alien" schools, except with special permission of the Department of Education, permission which could only be given for very serious reasons.[32] For a school to qualify as a "national" school and to accept Indonesian citizens as pupils, it must 1) follow the plan of instruction set down by the Department of Education and Culture; 2) be operated by a Board of Directors., all of whom were Indonesian citizens; and 3) have only Indonesian citizens as teachers.[33] A number of regulations in late 1957 also limited and restricted the alien (non-"national") schools. Not only were they limited to foreign children, they had also to prove that all their pupils were *not* Indonesian citizens. (This is probably the only case in Indonesian government practice in which

---

30 The Department of Education and Culture has published a white paper on alien schools, in cooperation with the military. See Departemen Pendidikan, Pengadjaran dan Kebudajaan bersama Staf Penguasa Perang Pusat, *Pengawasan pengadjaranasing* (Djakarta: c. 1959).

31 *Ibid.*, p. 28. Text of the order given in appendix VII of ibid.

32 *Ibid.*, appendix VIII. (As of 1962, even these permissions, given to children of Indonesian diplomats recently returned from abroad to attend English-language international schools in Djakarta, were withdrawn.)

33 These and subsequent regulations are contained in the appendices to the white paper referred to above.

a Chinese is assumed to be a citizen unless he can prove he is an alien.) Alien schools could only be established in about 150 cities throughout the archipelago; those in other towns and villages had to be closed. Not only the directors, but all the teachers had to pass an examination in writing and speaking Indonesian, and Indonesian language and history had to be taught. No visas would be issued to admit new foreign teachers unless it could be shown that there was no Indonesian citizen who could handle the job.

The Department of Education estimates that between November 1957 and July 1958 the number of alien schools was reduced from about 2000 to about 850, and the number of pupils from about 425,000 to 150,000. 250,000 of those displaced were Indonesian citizens. The number of cities and towns with alien schools declined from 750 to 158.

In April 1958 Indonesia began also to attack the activities of the Kuomintang. The PK1 had played a part in initiating the campaign when it produced evidence that Taiwan had been aiding the rebellion in Sumatra. The army subsequently took up the attack against Kuomintang businesses and organizations which were seized or forced to close, and all Chinese language newspapers were shut down.

During this campaign, all Kuomintang Chinese schools were closed and their property confiscated. Dutch-language schools had been closed after December 1957 when Indonesia seized Dutch-owned enterprises during the West Irian dispute. The net result, in January 1959, was that about 510 Chinese schools (of an original 1800), 15 Dutch-language schools (of 125), and 25 English-language schools (of 75) remained in operation in 150 places with 125,000 students. Of 1450 buildings formerly used by alien schools, about 1200 were taken over for "national" Indonesian schools. Although some instruction in Chinese was permitted during the transition period, the schools were expected to be fully Indonesian after 1960. No foreign language may now be taught at the elementary level in any national school.[34]

Most of the children who were forced to move were placed in national schools, frequently in the same buildings that had previously housed the alien schools. In Java and Bali at least, the Baperki branches took over the

---

34 *Ibid.*, appendix VIII.

operation of what were once Chinese schools.

In Nusatenggara, Baperki's response to the closures had been almost immediate. Before May 1957 they had sponsored schools in a number of places in Java, and Siauw had proposed as early as October 1956 that Baperki's first step in popularizing the Indonesian language among Chinese would be through the establishment of schools.[35] In Tanggerang, Tjilamaja (West Java), and Kediri, schools had been set up in 1956; in the latter a secondary school was opened. Baperki opened both an elementary and secondary school in Kudus in August 1957, before the alien school closings began in Java. Thus it seemed natural that Baperki should attempt to provide for the children displaced from alien schools, and by September 1957, four months after schools were ordered closed in Nusatenggara, a Baperki-sponsored educational foundation had begun its work in Bali. In Krawang, Tjirebon, Probolinggo, Ponorogo, Ngandjuk, Tulungagung and Tandjungkarang (South Sumatra), Baperki provided for the transferred students, frequently in cooperation with the directors of the alien schools and with the interest of representatives of China.[36] These schools today are Indonesian in curriculum but almost all are Chinese in student body; they parallel the prewar Dutch-Chinese schools which offered a Dutch curriculum to Chinese students. These new national schools may, if they wish, accept alien Chinese as well as citizens. Indonesian children are accepted (in Kediri they constitute 70 per cent of the students enrolled in one Baperki school),[37] but ordinarily they are only a tiny minority of the students.

Baperki runs perhaps 100 schools[38] throughout Indonesia; the large majority of them are in Java. In Djakarta alone it directs 14 elementary schools, 7 junior, and 3 senior high schools with a total of nearly 15,000 pupils.[39] Baperki also operates schools in a few places outside Java, and its leaders talk of expansion. In addition, it maintains a university in

---

35 *Republik*, 8 October 1956. This statement was made in Medan, where Chinese is commonly spoken, even among second or third generation Chinese. As of December 1962, however, Baperki had no schools of its own in Medan.

36 Based on accounts in *Republik* and *Berita Baperki*. This is clearly only a sampling of the schools erected both before and after 1957.

37 Interview 1963.

38 Interview 1963.

39 Jajasan Pendidikan dan Kebudajaan Baperki, *Pekan karja peladjar Baperki* (program) (Djakarta, July 1962).

Djakarta with a branch in Surabaja. Although the university has a good staff (many of the instructors teach also at the University of Indonesia) and facilities, its degrees in 1963 were not yet recognized by the Indonesian government, (The decision about recognizing the degrees may well have been postponed until Baperki University has its first graduates.) In recent years, Indonesian state universities have followed a policy of giving preference to children of government employees, very few of whom are Chinese. In practice, at the University of Indonesia in Djakarta, Chinese are limited to about 10 per cent of the enrollment in certain faculties such as law and medicine, and in many other state-supported faculties, they find it difficult to obtain admission.

Baperki an educational organization in traditional pattern

Even if Baperki were merely an educational organization, it would be performing a necessary and welcome service to the Chinese, especially the *peranakans*. *Peranakan* values emphasize education, and the Indonesian government-run schools cannot yet meet their demands. For years, the preference for liberal professions has been marked among the *peranakans*: Baperki University's first faculties were those of medicine, law, dentistry, and engineering, all popular professions among the *peranakan* Chinese. The educational services provided by Baperki are not limited to the Chinese who are Indonesian citizens (neither are they limited to Chinese). Aliens may enter the schools, and, in Baperki University, graduates of the Chinese-language schools, who are not ordinarily accepted by state universities, may be admitted for study. Admission of graduates from the Chinese-language schools is an important concession to the alien group, for these students, before 1961, had to go outside of Indonesia, to China, Hong Kong, or Singapore, to continue their education.

Not only the subject matter, but the Baperki educational philosophy is a *peranakan* one; thus, it emphasizes five principles (*Pantja Tjinta*; literally five loves): love of one's country and the people, love of humanity and peace, love of work, love of science and culture, and love of one's parents.[40] (This is a parody of the Indonesian national *Pantjasila* or the

---

40 *Ibid.*

five principles of the Indonesian state.) Both "love of work" and "love of one's parents" could be said to be particularly important values to *peranakan* Chinese.

Not only is Baperki's educational activity valuable and, in the eyes of many Chinese, necessary; it is also traditional. Since the *Tiong Hoa Hwe Koan* was established in 1900, Chinese schools have been a central concern of both the *peranakan* and *totok* segments of the Chinese community. In fulfilling this need in the community for an educational foundation, Baperki is following in the footsteps of predecessor organizations among the Chinese in Java and elsewhere which likewise founded schools as part of their service to the community.

CHAPTER TWO

DUAL CITIZENSHIP SETTLED, 1959-1962

The dual citizenship treaty, which had been ratified by both China and Indonesia in December 1957, was not implemented until January 1960. This coincided with Indonesia's prohibition of retail trade by aliens in small towns and rural areas, which was carried out in late 1959 and early 1960. The ban against alien trade in rural areas was a severe attack on the economic position of the alien Chinese, causing repercussions among the citizen Chinese which in turn affected their attitude to Indonesia and to dual citizenship.

Alien retail ban and its effect

On May 14, 1959, the Minister of Trade, Rachmat Muljomiseno, issued a regulation forbidding all retail trade by aliens outside of the capital towns of first- and second-level autonomous areas to take effect January 1, 1960. There were twenty-two first-level autonomous areas: the twenty provinces, the city of Djakarta, and the special region of Jogjakarta. In Java, there were eighty-three second-level autonomous areas (including the three provincial capitals). In other words, aliens could do retail business in about eighty-five cities and towns in Java and in about 120 outside of Java.[1]

The regulation attacked the traditional Chinese role as middleman in gathering agricultural products for the towns or for export and in the distribution of city-made or imported goods in rural areas. It is

---

1 List of autonomous areas from J.D. Legge, *Central Authority and Regional Autonomy in Indonesia* (Ithaca, N. Y.: Cornell University Press, 1961), pp. 247-255, and Lembaga Administrasi Negara, *Ichtisar perkembangan otonomi daerah* (Djakarta: Djambatan, 1960), pp. 124-141.

significant that the Minister concerned came from the Nahdatul Ulama party, a party of conservative Moslems with considerable support among Indonesian small traders in the rural areas of Java, especially East Java. (We do not know to what extent other members of the cabinet supported this regulation.) These traders might look forward to a chance of opening up new businesses in place of the Chinese. Nor was it coincidental that the ban was announced in May 1959 at a meeting of "national" (non-Chinese) businessmen, a group that the new regulation was meant to favor. Furthermore, the alien retail ban was passed a month after the exclusion of private businessmen from most of the import trade, where national businessmen had previously enjoyed special privileges.[2]

Because of the emergency laws then in effect, the local military commanders were responsible for implementing the ban. On August 28, 1959 the commander of West Java issued a military regulation requiring all aliens to leave the rural[3] areas by December 31. The reason given was the uncertainty of security conditions in his area.[4] It is interesting to compare this regulation with the old Dutch laws confining Chinese residence to special quarters. One important difference is that, under the Dutch, a Chinese with business in the rural areas was often exempted from the residence restrictions, and, at least for some time, one who owned a substantial house or other property outside the prescribed quarter for Chinese could remain in it.[5] Thus the Dutch tolerated Chinese business interests and Indonesia, by the terms of this regulation, did not.

In November 1959, the original ban and the subsequent military regulations were combined and modified slightly by Presidential Regulation (*Peraturan Presiden*, abbreviated PP-10) Number 10/1959. The new regulation upheld the original prohibition of ordinary retail trade, but allowed aliens to remain in the rural areas unless the regional military commander, in the interests of security, required them to move. They might still engage in one of seventeen small business activities specifically

---

2   J.A.C. Mackie, "The Chinese in Indonesia," *Australia's Neighbors*, No. 102, December 1959.

3   "Rural" is used hereafter to refer to areas outside the capitals of second-level autonomous areas, that is, those covered by the alien retail ban.

4   PIA, 23 October 1959. The ban was dated August 28. The Darul Islam rebellion had disturbed West Java's security for some years.

5   Brokx, *op. cit.*, p. 31.

permitted to aliens in the rural areas. These included transportation, catering, hairdressing, dentistry, and a number of other occupations[6] in which the Chinese do participate actively; however, any additional opportunities in these fields could not have offered an alternative to all the displaced Chinese retailers in rural areas.

The new regulation also attempted to answer critics of the original ban by placing it in the context of Indonesian socialism. The alien businesses were to be replaced, where possible, by cooperative endeavors (which might, in turn, employ the displaced Chinese). Only if the cooperatives were unable to take over would "national businessmen" be free to do so, This appeal to "Socialism," however, seems to have been no more than a rationalization, as the cooperative organizations then existing in Indonesia were far too weak to replace all alien Chinese retailers,

A number of military commanders in the Outer Islands — South Kalimantan, South and Southeast Sulawesi, and parts of Sumatra — also prohibited alien residence in rural areas. In most of these areas, in contrast to West Java, the Chinese were already living in the towns,[7] East and Central Java's military commanders allowed the alien Chinese to remain where they were. West Java's military commanders began in late 1959 to force the Chinese to leave rural areas.

Response of Chinese community

What of the effects of the ban so far as the Chinese themselves were concerned? According to a government estimate, 25,000 shops were affected throughout Indonesia.[8] A report on the Indonesian population at the end of 1957[9] listed 71, 233 alien Chinese in the "rural" areas of Java, out of a total of 383, 931 alien and 625, 356 citizen Chinese in all Java. Of these rural aliens, 15, 600 were in West Java — where all were required

---

6 Mackie, *op. cit.*; text of PP-10 in PIA, 19 November 1959.
7 The ban on Chinese rural residence in South and Southeast Sulawesi actually preceded that in West Java and the deadline for moving was September 31, 1959. (PIA, 7 August 1959). However, because of the administrative reorganization of South Sulawesi, most of the towns where alien Chinese lived were second-level autonomous area capitals anyway. (Interview, 1963) The same is true of South Kalimantan, where very few Chinese live in rural areas.
8 Statement of Minister of Distribution Leimena, *Pedoman*, 6 January 1960.
9 Biro Pusat Statistik, *Penduduk Indonesia* 1957. See p. 2, note 5 for explanation of how these figures were derived.

to move to larger towns — 12,000 in Central Java, and 44,000 in East Java. This meant that there was a minimum of perhaps 12,000 Chinese households in rural Java (allowing six persons per household), a large percentage of which would have been engaged in retail trade.

To assume that the effects of PP-10 were the same throughout Indonesia as they were in West Java would be to overestimate them considerably. Outside of Java, the alien residence ban seems to have been implemented in areas where the Chinese actually were concentrated in the cities, such as in South Kalimantan or South Sulawesi, and not where the majority of the Chinese were rural-dwellers, as in West Kalimantan. The alien Chinese shops in West Kalimantan have been closed, however. Similarly, although alien retail trade was forbidden in the rural areas of East and Central Java, aliens were not required to move to the cities. This argues that, except in West Java, aliens were required to move from rural areas only in provinces where few aliens lived in rural areas anyway.

The effects of the ban should not be minimized, however, for it extended to both the *totok* and *peranakan* communities. According to the Bureau of Statistics of Indonesia, 102, 297 Chinese left the country in 1960. (In a normal year, only about 12,000 would migrate.[10]) Many were displaced shopkeepers and their families, but many, perhaps one-third or more, were not, From the dispatches of the New China News Agency (Peking), which gave the matter considerable attention up to August 1960, it is clear that a sizeable proportion were high school and college students. There were several cases, usually well-publicized, of prominent *peranakan* Chinese departing for the mainland, but an overwhelming majority of the emigrants were *totok* Chinese, most of the older ones born in China. One of the ships which left from Djakarta in April 1960 carried 1500 Chinese, over half of whom, described as "poverty-stricken," were not from rural areas but from the city itself. Fires in the Chinese settlements in Pemangkat (West Kalimantan) and Selat Pandjang (Riau archipelago, Central Sumatra) caused several thousand to apply to "return" to China. For all of these, as for coffee growers in Bali who had previously been deprived of their land or for miners in Belitung thrown out of work when tin mining declined, the alien ban was less a cause of their decision to go

---

10 Biro Pusat Statistik, *Statistical Pocketbook of Indonesia 1961* (Djakarta, c. 1962), p. 15,

to China than an opportunity to do something they had been hoping to do for some time.

Of the first 40,000 repatriates, 10,000 came from West Java (probably including Djakarta).[11] In all, perhaps 50-60 per cent of the emigrants were from Java, the rest from Sumatra, Kalimantan, Sulawesi, Bali and Lombok. The Chinese government had sent ships to collect the returnees. Later, the Indonesian military also hired vessels for this purpose, In West Kalimantan, according to local Chinese concerned with the problem, a number of people who were stranded when China stopped sending ships to pick up returnees finally were settled on a plot of uncultivated land by the Indonesian government.[12]

Outside of West Java, where there was less pressure and publicity, it was easier to reach some accommodation with the authorities, particularly if the Chinese were not forced to move. It must be emphasized that the ban was directed against *alien* retail trade; thus Chinese who were Indonesian citizens were supposedly unaffected. Nevertheless, since at that time they had no documentary proof of citizenship, some citizen Chinese were forced to close their businesses. On the other hand, it was sometimes possible for a Chinese to reopen his business after obtaining proof of Indonesian citizenship or by transferring title to a member of his family who was a citizen (although theoretically this was not legal). Even in West Java, in 1962, there was talk of Chinese "going back" to the rural areas from which they had been expelled; in many cases, these must have been those who were later able to prove their Indonesian citizenship in the course of implementation of the dual citizenship treaty. Military authorities in that area in 1962 or 1963 also permitted some alien Chinese to continue their businesses in rural areas, although they were expected to reside in the towns. (This is a nice parallel to the Dutch residence restrictions mentioned above, and in this case, the Chinese were allowed concessions for economic reasons.)

11 Based on New China News Agency English-language dispatches, 1960.
12 Interview, 1963.

Effects of the ban on Indonesia

What of the effect of the ban on Indonesia as a whole? The Chinese retailers in the course of decades had developed a system of buying crops on advance loans, and although this practice frequently led to exploitation of the farmers, it was still in 1959 an essential part of marketing and distribution in Indonesia, Since neither cooperatives nor national businessmen were fully equipped to replace the Chinese, or at least to do business with equal efficiency, the ban resulted in considerable economic disruption. In the short run, the ban did more harm than good to the villagers it was supposed to help,

But it also had effects beyond the rural areas, undermining the confidence of Chinese shopkeepers in the cities, particularly when it was proposed that the prohibition of alien trade be extended to the cities. The inventories of Chinese shops in Djakarta vanished from the shelves, for the owners feared that their businesses might also be confiscated. Eventually, normalcy was achieved, but at the cost of higher prices, lower standards, or tacitly allowing the Chinese to return to business.

West Java: a special situation

Since so much attention was focused on West Java at the time of the alien retail ban, it merits extra comment. The 15, 600 alien Chinese in its rural areas were not evenly distributed throughout the province. According to the figures in *Penduduk Indonesia* for 1957, only about 500 aliens lived in rural areas to the west of Djakarta, in Tanggerang, and in the Bantam residency, (Several hundred ethnic Chinese live in rural areas in Tanggerang, but they have been there for generations and are not aliens.) About 1500 alien Chinese lived in the east of West Java, in the Tjirebon residency. The potential trouble spots, in implementing the regulation requiring aliens to move to larger towns, were Bekasi-Krawang-Purwakarta, with 3000 aliens, and the Bogor-Priangan axis: Bogor residency, including Sukabumi and Tjiandjur, with 3700 aliens and Priangan with 6900 (4800 of which lived in rural areas close to the city of Bandung). These were, in fact, the areas where incidents occurred in the course of implementing the alien ban.

What are some of the social factors making for bad relations between Chinese and Indonesians in West Java? When parts of Krawang and Bekasi came under the old private lands system, some Chinese had been able to acquire substantial tracts of land in the area, and this may well be at the root of some Indonesian resentment. Along the Bogor-Priangan axis, however, there is another factor of importance. In 1925, the Priangan residency was the home of one-third of the substantial native landowners of Java and Madura, that is, over 1200 persons with individual landholdings of over 17.7 hectares (one hectare = about 2.5 acres).[13]

These, like all Sundanese, a re strongly Islamic; furthermore, the Islamic teachers of the area belong, or are closely connected, to the group of landowners and businessmen.[14] Since the common people are also strongly Islamic, at times to the point of fanaticism (as the area's support for the Darul Islam rebellion shows), their religious leaders hold a much more influential social position than do their counterparts in most of East and Central Java. These leaders look with greatest distaste on the Chinese, who are their business competitors, in addition to being of a different religion. This attitude might be extended to many of the military in West Java, for they too are usually Sundanese. (For example, the West Java commander who passed the alien residence ban, Colonel Kosasih, is from Sukabumi.)

On the other hand, in Sunda, there has not grown up, as there has in East and Central Java, especially Jogjakarta and Solo, a class of Chinese *peranakans* who are strongly attracted to the indigenous culture. These Javanese areas produced Chinese *peranakan* devotees of Javanese music and opera, as well as a tradition of intermarriage between wealthy Chinese and Javanese aristocratic families. Although there is ample evidence of some acculturation among the *peranakan* Chinese in the Sundanese areas,[15] this has been more superficial, perhaps because of the

---

13 Scheltema, *Deelbouw in Nederlandsch-Indië* (Wageningen, 1931), p. 275, cited in Karl J, Pelzer, *Pioneer Settlement in the Asiatic Tropics* (New York: American Geographical Society, 1948), p. 257.

14 Soelaeman Soemardi, *Regional Politicians and Administrators in West Java, 1956* (M.A. Thesis, Cornell University, 1961), pp. 75-87 treats of this.

15 For a study of Chinese acculturation in a Sundanese area, see Giok-Lan Tan, *The Chinese of Sukabumi* (Ithaca, N. Y.: Cornell Modern Indonesia Project, 1963).

pervasiveness of Islam (which the Chinese have not found attractive), perhaps for reasons inherent in the Sundanese culture itself.

One final factor, of considerable importance in the 1959-60 incidents, is the fact that certain Chinese communities were located on major roads, easily accessible from Djakarta. Members of the Chinese Embassy in Djakarta toured West Java to encourage the Chinese there to resist evacuation from rural areas. The Chinese side, like the Indonesian, was not devoid of fanaticism.

Dual citizenship treaty goes into effect

The effect of the alien retail policy on relations between Indonesia and the People's Republic of China was nearly disastrous. It seems clear that President Soekarno ultimately intervened to lessen the severity of attacks on the Chinese, both by the concessions offered in PP-10 and in subsequent negotiations with Chinese authorities. In an effort to salvage something of amicable relations, the two countries finally agreed to exchange instruments of ratification of the dual citizenship treaty, in Peking, on January 20, 1960. (Both countries had ratified the treaty some three years previously, but it had not yet gone into effect.)

On Peking's part, this conciliatory attitude may have been an attempt to woo Indonesia's support against India in the Sino-Indian border dispute then brewing. Perhaps she wished to force Indonesia to implement the article of the treaty guaranteeing protection of the rights of Chinese citizens. At any rate, Chinese who were considered Indonesian citizens had two years in which to make a court declaration rejecting their Chinese citizenship. If they failed to appear in court, they would be considered as Chinese citizens and have lost their right to Indonesian citizenship.[16]

---

16 For details of the treaty, see Willmott, *National Status, op. cit.*. The reader is reminded that the treaty applied only to persons who were already Indonesian citizens. Should they lose their Indonesian citizenship by failing to reject Chinese citizenship, they could regain it only by becoming naturalized. Provisions for minors were more complicated; if their parents were regarded as Indonesian citizens in 1960, they were allowed one year after their coming of age in which to make a decision on citizenship; otherwise they would follow the choice of their parents in 1960-62. Children of aliens born after 1949 were aliens. Special provisions were eventually worked out for children born before 1949 in Indonesia whose parents had rejected their own or their children's Indonesian citizenship in 1949-51; see pp. 31 and 35. Children born after 1960 follow their parents. In Indonesia, a person under 18 and unmarried is a minor.

Exemptions from the treaty: Chinese-Indonesian negotiations

The Chou En-lai — Ali Sastroamidjojo notes had provided that some citizen Chinese could be exempt from making the choice and yet still be considered Indonesian citizens. On the ground of these notes, Indonesia had unilaterally made a number of exceptions (contained in Government Regulation Number 20/1959). These applied to members and former members of national and regional representative bodies, the armed forces or the police; present or former government or regional employees; those who had represented Indonesia abroad more than once in politics, economics, culture or sport and had not subsequently represented China; and any farmer whose way of life in Indonesian society, in the opinion of the Ministers of Internal Affairs, Justice and Agrarian Affairs, shows that he is really a native.[17]

Nevertheless, a joint committee of members from China and Indonesia, meeting in Djakarta, was to formulate a supplementary agreement on implementation of the treaty. Only in October 1960 was agreement reached, and it was signed in December. Implementation could therefore not proceed until nearly half the implementation period of two years had expired.[18]

Two major points had divided the Chinese and Indonesian committee members. The delegates from China had favored the widest and most lenient interpretation of the treaty. First they argued for the exemption of all electors from making the choice, on the grounds that voting indicated their loyalty to Indonesia; second, they supported a provision (also proposed by Siauw Giok Tjhan of Baperki) which would allow Indonesia-born Chinese who had been minors in the 1949-51 period of choice and whose parents had rejected Indonesian citizenship — and who had therefore lost Indonesian citizenship involuntarily — to become Indonesian citizens by filing a declaration within one year of their coming of age. An attempt had been made to implement the latter provision in

---

17 Text of regulation in *ibid.*, p. 138.

18 The story of the negotiations is contained in Susanto Tirtoprodjo, Hasil-kerdja Panitya Bersama (Djakarta: Djambatan, 1961), For an early analysis of the implementation, see also David Mozingo, "The Sino-Indonesian Dual Nationality Treaty," Asian Survey, December 1961, NCNA announced the agreement in September 1960.

1958 (ending August 1, 1959), but without much success because the Indonesian courts had been unwilling, or unable, to deal promptly with the matter.[19]

Not only did the representatives of China argue for these exceptions, they wanted all persons of Chinese descent born in Indonesia to have the option of choosing Indonesian citizenship, irrespective of whether they had previously rejected it,[20] Thus, China's attitude was in contrast to her traditional claim to the loyalty of all persons of Chinese descent. In this she was, of course, actually defending the interest of these Chinese, for she recognized, as did Baperki, that it would be most desirable from their point of view to have Indonesian citizenship.

The Indonesian members of the joint committee (one of them was actually of Chinese descent, Lie Po Yu, a PNI member of the *Gotong-Rojong* Parliament, but he was not an influential political figure) argued for the strictest possible interpretation of eligibility for Indonesian citizenship. Since the Indonesian Chinese had no vigorous spokesman on the Indonesian delegation, they needed the help of the Chinese officials. Baperki and members of the Chinese Embassy were thus working in cooperation for a lenient interpretation of who might be an Indonesian citizen.

Even after the joint committee had reached agreement, the Indonesian cabinet refused to accept the provision allowing option of citizenship to all those who had lost Indonesian citizenship as minors in 1949-51. Cabinet members expressed the fear that this would allow those youths who had been educated and "indoctrinated" in China to return to Indonesia. Settlement only came when President Soekarno intervened personally on behalf of the Chinese viewpoint, emphasizing that friendship with China was more important than these trivial considerations. (In this, the President was repeating his earlier intervention on behalf of the alien Chinese retailers.) Nevertheless, Foreign Minister Subandrio persuaded Chinese Ambassador Huang Chen to agree that the concession was meant only for those youths who had remained in Indonesia.[21]

---

19 Column on citizenship, *Star Weekly*, 5 September 1959; Susanto, *op. cit.*, p. 6.
20 Susanto, *op. cit.*, p.14.
21 *Ibid.*, pp. 17-19.

Implementation of the treaty

What of the implementation of the choice? Although only a few months remained for actual choosing, the evidence suggests that virtually all persons affected by the treaty were aware of it and had some idea of the effect which loss of Indonesian citizenship would have on their interests. A good deal of the credit for spreading information about citizenship goes to Baperki.

Actually, implementation of choices could have begun before final agreement was reached by the joint committee in December 1960, and in some places it did. Any declarations processed before the protocol on implementation was signed (that is, those made under the terms of Indonesian Government Regulation 20/1959) were declared legal, provided they were not in conflict with the joint committee's agreement.[22] However, because of lack of understanding and cooperation on the part of Indonesian officials, few, if any, applications could have been processed before December 1960.

Assessment of the effect of implementation on citizen Chinese requires consideration of the various provisions and exemptions. First, the original exemption of regulation 20/1959 would probably have covered only a few thousand persons. Perhaps a few hundred Chinese have ever served in some representative body in Indonesia; Chinese members of police are virtually nonexistent, although the military draft has brought some Chinese into the armed forces. Again, although some of Indonesia's best athletes are of Chinese descent, only a few Chinese could claim to have represented Indonesia abroad. The clause allowing present or former government employees to be Indonesian citizens was more meaningful. Although *peranakan* Chinese traditionally avoided government service, several thousand are probable included in this category now: doctors, lawyers, economists, employees of former Dutch firms now under Indonesian government ownership, and others.

The exemption of farmers could have been quite significant, not only because 10 to 15 per cent of the Indonesian Chinese[23] might be covered by

---

22 *Ibid.*, p. 19.
23 *Volkstelling 1930*, Volume VII, Subsidiary Table 26, says 10 per cent of local-born Chinese with a profession in Java, 11 per cent in Sumatra, and 32 per cent of those elsewhere were ordinary

it, but because this was just the group which would find the court process most difficult. However, in practice, the exemption seems to have affected no one. In West Kalimantan, no farmers were exempted because their social position was not considered comparable to that of the indigenous Indonesians. Indeed, Chinese farmers in that area can hardly be called "Indonesians"; most cannot speak the Indonesian language. In places like Tanggerang, where farmers of Chinese descent live much as Indonesians do, and speak Indonesian as their daily language, many of the farmers had already made other arrangements by the time the conditions allowing them exemptions were published. A Chinese farmer who could be considered "indigenous" must, in addition to speaking Indonesian (or an Indonesian language) daily and participating in village activities, earn his income from working the soil. Many Chinese farmers in the Tanggerang area would be disqualified because a major source of their income comes from supplementary trading, the raising and selling of pigs, for example, or from renting out their land.

The problem of farmers was also complicated by the Agrarian Law then being put into effect. Most, if not all, of the Chinese farmers in Java held land under old titles of ownership (*eigendom*). The new law would convert them either to new ownership titles (*hak milik*), which were reserved for citizens only, or to twenty-year leases (*hak guna bangunan*, literally building rights). For owners who could not prove that they held *only* Indonesian citizenship on September 24, 1960, the land would be converted to lease rights.[24] Since the dual citizenship treaty was not really implemented by that time, Chinese farmers have attempted to use the exemptions to the treaty as a way to secure ownership of their land. Since they did not qualify as only Indonesian citizens, however, some Chinese farmers have instead tried to use the fact that they voted to claim that they held only Indonesian citizenship on September 24, 1960. (In Tanggerang, where Baperki has been rather active, partly because it is so convenient to Djakarta, many Chinese farmers did vote in 1955 or

---

"native" farmers.

24 Text of laws in Gouw Giok Siong, *Tafsiran Undang2 Pokok Agraria* (Djakarta: Keng Po, 1960), especially pp. 195-196. Susanto, *op. cit.* p. 22, recognizes that this regulation conflicts with the dual citizenship provisions but argues that since the Agrarian Law is *lex specialis*, it takes precedence in this matter. In the author's opinion, the reverse is true because, on the matter of citizenship, the treaty and not the Agrarian Law is the definitive law.

1957.) In Tanggerang, local authorities refused to accept this argument, but reportedly a few Chinese in Central Java were able to take advantage of this escape clause.[25]

The exemption of voters from having to make a court declaration was potentially of greatest importance in the implementation of the dual citizenship treaty. Many voters, however, still preferred to go through the normal court-declaration procedure, regarding it as more certain. Scattered figures made available by Baperki in 1962 indicate that the number of Chinese who took advantage of any exemption was probably less than a third of the total who made a decision. The exemption of voters does still remain important, for, like the other exemptions listed above, it has no time limit. Thus a person might still be considered an Indonesian citizen if he could prove that he voted legally in 1955 or 1957, even though he made no decision in the 1960-62 choice period. In practice, however, nearly all those who took the trouble to vote also took the trouble to do something about their citizenship.

Baperki active in implementation; evaluation of treaty's effects

For most Indonesian citizen Chinese, the treaty implementation meant going to court to choose Indonesian citizenship. Baperki officials estimate that 70 to 90 per cent of those eligible elected Indonesian citizenship in this or other ways; government officials say 65 per cent. For those who had difficulty collecting the proper documents (birth and marriage certificates, etc.) or were uncertain about procedures, Baperki, the Sin Ming Hui, or civic-minded individuals set up committees where, for a nominal fee (Rp 35 to 100, at most), a person could obtain legal aid. In many areas, such as South Kalimantan, these committees sent persons to isolated parts of the province to inform people of the provisions of the treaty. Understandably, these committees often knew more about the citizenship regulations than did the Indonesian officials responsible. In one provincial capital, when a paper shortage delayed implementation,

---

25 Interview, 1963. The meaning of the farmer-exemption or voter-exemption in implementation of the dual citizenship treaty was that such persons held no citizenship but Indonesian and therefore did not have to reject Chinese citizenship. It was hoped that this could qualify these persons under the Agrarian Law as thus holding *only* Indonesian citizenship in September 1960.

Baperki paid for the printing of the necessary forms; in another, when a fire destroyed the court's records, Baperki provided its duplicate copies of the previous transactions.

Much depended on the good will and expertise of the local officials. In at least two places, all the early choices were recorded on the wrong forms and had to be filled out again. Elsewhere, as in parts of East Java, judges insisted on having the father's birth certificate, as well as that of the person choosing, an impossible condition to fulfill, since Chinese births were not required to be registered in Java until 1919 and elsewhere until 1926. Once the court declaration was completed, papers were passed on to the capital for approval. Djakarta Justice Department officials were particularly fussy; the forms of some applicants were returned three times for minor corrections before they were finally certified.

One factor which favored the Chinese, many of whom waited until late in 1961 to register their choice, was that it was not necessary for the declaration to be fully processed or even for the person to have appeared in court, before January 20, 1962. So long as his intent to choose Indonesian citizenship had been registered with the court, he might take the actual oath months later and still be secure in his citizenship. Even in late 1962, many Chinese who had actively chosen Indonesian citizenship had therefore not yet completed the processing of their applications.

Balanced against this was the tendency on the part of Djakarta officials to reject applications for the slightest technical error, These were, however, usually returned to the person concerned for changes, and very few were rejected completely. Theoretically, in the case of a flat and final rejection from the Justice Department, the person concerned has the right to appeal to the joint committee on implementation, which represents China and Indonesia. But this committee has not actually met since 1960, although the protocol to the treaty had envisaged it as a continuing body to deal with such appeals.

Finally, the manner of implementation of the provision for those who were under age in 1949-51 whose parents had then rejected Indonesian citizenship has virtually rendered it a dead letter. Those concerned must prove that they did not leave Indonesia after 1949 or, if they left the country, that they did not leave without a re-entry permit nor stay abroad longer than the permit allowed. As of late 1962, implementation of this was stalled because the immigration officials in Indonesia were unable or unwilling to certify that these requirements had been met. As chairman Siauw of Baperki said in November 1962, "Thousands of youths must wait for the completion of their forms which still cannot be finished by our officials."[26] The youths must make their choice within one year of their coming of age.

Of course the choice of citizenship on the part of many Chinese was motivated by self-interest. A typical attitude, expressed by one *peranakan* in late 1962, was:

"I was born in Indonesia and I will be buried here. I can't speak Chinese, and even if I went to China, I couldn't adjust to the life there. So why not be an Indonesian citizen?"

The effect of PP-10 on the *peranakan* Chinese was not only to emphasize that to become Indonesian citizens was in their economic interest. Reports soon reached Indonesia of bad conditions prevailing in China and even the Peking government itself is reported to have discouraged more Chinese from applying to return (or rather, to go) to China, Flight to China was no longer possible for disaffected *peranakans*. The events of 1959-1960 forced the Indonesian Chinese to think more realistically about their future in Indonesia and about the disadvantages of being aliens in the land which was, after all, their home.

---

26 Siauw Giok Tjhan, *Pantja Sila anti-rasialisme* (Baperki, n. p., c. 1962), p. 40.

CHAPTER THREE

THE DEBATE ON ASSIMILATION

Discussion within the peranakan Chinese community about a solution to the minority problem has now polarized around two viewpoints. Baperki has favored "integration" which would allow the peranakan Chinese to retain their identity within Indonesian society. A second group has favored assimilation, the disappearance of the Chinese as a separate group.

Baperki's view: integration

Baperki's point of view, summarized under the term "integration" (*integrasi*), is that the Chinese who are Indonesian citizens should be accepted as a group into Indonesian society. Thus, they put the burden of acceptance on the Indonesian majority, while at the same time emphasizing the need for citizenship education of the Chinese.

Since its earliest days, Baperki's leadership has advocated some solution to the minority question within this essentially conservative framework, In 1957, they sponsored a conference on the potential contribution of citizens of foreign descent to Indonesian culture. Boejoeng Saleh, who was then chairman of the cultural section of Baperki, spoke for integration of the Chinese, Eurasian, and Arab minorities into Indonesian society, arguing that no provision of Indonesia's Constitution required them to disappear.[1]

---

1 *Simposion Baperki tentang: sumbangsih apakah jang dapat diberikan oleh warganegara2 Indonesia keturunan asing kepada pembinaan dan perkem-bangan kebudajaan nasional Indonesia* (Djakarta: Baperki, 1957), pp. 9-16.

Ambivalent attitude toward Chinese traditions

Although it calls for training *peranakans* to be good citizens of Indonesia, Baperki's attitude toward the *perpetuation* of Chinese traditions could be called "ambivalent." Should *peranakans* be encouraged to appreciate Indonesian culture or should they be taught that of mainland China? In recent years, Baperki's cultural programs have often given considerable attention to peculiarly Indonesian presentations. This is partly a matter of *peranakan* taste in the various regions. Thus, in parts of Java, Baperki directly or indirectly sponsors wajang orang performances, a Javanese entertainment which is popular among *peranakans* in Central and East Java. Where Javanese influence is less among *peranakans*, as in Djakarta, a cultural program might feature mainland Chinese folk songs and dances as well. In contrast, at Baperki University, where the faculty of arts offers Chinese, Indonesian, and English language and literature for study, it is English which is the overwhelming favorite. Practical young *peranakans* are choosing, therefore, a widely-spoken and used language, English, rather than either Chinese or Indonesian studies. Perhaps the choice of English also indicates *peranakan* preference for Western education; Chinese studies, the sentimental favorite, takes second place, and Indonesian literature is least favored by the students.

Baperki's dental faculty aroused a protest when it included the study of the Chinese language in its curriculum. Its answer was that many of the students might wish to continue their study in China because dentistry was so advanced there.[2] As was mentioned above, graduates of the Chinese-language secondary schools may be admitted to the University.

When it promotes Chinese language and contemporary mainland culture, Baperki is not reinforcing something which already exists among *peranakans* but introducing new elements. So far, however, this has been less important in Baperki's activities than the promotion of specifically *peranakan* or Indonesian cultural activities. These cultural considerations, indicating a certain ambivalence *vis à vis* Chinese or

---

2   Dr. Jetty Rizali Noor, "Perguruan tinggi swastapun harus 'terpimpin,'" *Star Weekly*, 24 October 1959.

Indonesian culture, are but the background for Baperki's more political statements on "integration."

Since its inception Baperki has emphasized the need to fight against discrimination in Indonesian life. The very choice of the word "integration" was an attempt to identify their cause with that of the Negro in the United States, although the analogy with that minority group breaks down at once on both historical and economic grounds.

Baperki refuses to accept the Indonesian argument that the Dutch colonial government consciously favored the Chinese in Indonesia, and that the only way to solve the resulting minority problem must be for Indonesia deliberately to discriminate against the Chinese minority, particularly in the economic and educational fields, in order to bring about a balance. Baperki admits that Indonesia has a minority who are wealthy, or "economically strong," and a majority who are "economically weak," but denies that this minority/majority division is simply a division between Chinese and Indonesian. In fact, many Indonesians are economically strong, for example some of the indigenous businessmen who have profited from government favoritism in the recent past, and many Chinese are economically weak, for example farmers or poverty-stricken laborers. Since these minority/majority divisions are a matter of class, and not of race, any solution to them cannot follow racial lines. Simply favoring Indonesians over Chinese will not eradicate minority/majority distinctions, but will aggravate them. Instead the government should favor all poor farmers and laborers as against monopoly capitalists of all races, especially the Europeans who have the strongest link with colonialism.

Peranakan Chinese as a "suku"

On the matter of the social and cultural future of the Chinese in Indonesia, Baperki advocates cultural pluralism, insisting that the *peranakan* Chinese can and will be good Indonesian citizens while remaining a culturally distinct group. The Indonesian motto, "Unity in Diversity" (*Bhinneka Tunggal Ika*), refers to the many ethnic groups (*sukus*) existing within the Indonesian nation. Indonesian citizens of Chinese descent should be considered no differently from any other *suku* in Indonesia and should be accepted on the same terms. Conceivably, in some distant future (which

Siauw identifies with the achievement of true Indonesian socialism) all *sukus* will disappear into one Indonesian ethnic group. Only then can the Chinese be expected to be assimilated into the Indonesian nation. Any expectation of earlier Chinese assimilation would be unfair and unrealistic.

These opinions, particularly as presented by Siauw on behalf of Baperki, take some of their inspiration from the national minority policies of the USSR and the People's Republic of China. Siauw seems to find it desirable that the Chinese in Indonesia achieve a legal status comparable to that of the Thai or Korean peoples in China, While the argument he makes is really one for cultural autonomy and equality of treatment, the analogy is hardly appropriate, for the national minorities in China and Russia (like the Indonesian *sukus*) occupy a territory of their own, something the Chinese in Indonesia neither have nor would conceivably want. Furthermore, the problem of these national minorities is not complicated by the presence of resident aliens who are also members of the minority group, as is that of the Chinese community in Indonesia. In the Soviet Union or China, all members of the minorities are regarded as Soviet or Chinese citizens.

The Baperki argument begins with the undesirability of discrimination against the citizen Chinese as a first premise and argues to a justification of their existence as a separate group, So far as the Indonesian Chinese themselves are concerned, it is a justification of the *status quo*, and hence a conservative theory.

Assimilation and opposition to Baperki

In 1959 and 1960, a small group of *peranakans* emerged who believed that the *status quo* itself was responsible for discrimination against the Chinese citizens of Indonesia. Accordingly, they formulated some ideas on assimilation (*assimilasi* or *asimilasi*) of the Chinese which stand in contrast to those of Baperki.

The assimilationist group blamed the Chinese themselves for bad relations with the Indonesians. It argued that, in addition to accepting Indonesian citizenship, the Chinese should participate more actively in Indonesian political and social life. Instead of despairing of Indonesia over the effects of PP-10, they should dissociate themselves from the fate of the alien Chinese and enter more into the Indonesian social scene. The assimilationists expressed disapproval of organizations and activities which were predominantly Chinese in membership and those in which citizen Chinese mixed with aliens, as in Baperki University. They urged the citizen Chinese to campaign for their acceptance by the Indonesian majority by adopting Indonesian-sounding names and by lowering the barriers against Chinese-Indonesian marriage. In other words, assimilation meant that the Chinese — at least those who had become Indonesian citizens — must cease to be culturally distinct from the Indonesian majority and must dissociate themselves from Chinese traditions.

The magazine *Star Weekly* attempted to popularize the idea of assimilation when it was first proposed. One of the earliest articles on the subject compared assimilation of Chinese in the Philippines with the existing situation in Indonesia, arguing that complete assimilation of persons of Chinese descent was a fact in the Philippines, and was therefore also possible in Indonesia.[3]

When publication of *Star Weekly* ceased in September 1961 (for reasons not connected with this debate), other young *peranakans* attempted to continue the movement. The discussion which had begun within the *peranakan*, citizen Chinese community soon took on political overtones. If assimilation was the desirable course, then such an organization as Baperki was unnecessary and even undesirable. Support of assimilation became for some an indirect way to attack Baperki, whose leadership was regarded as undesirably sympathetic to communism (because of its leaders' cooperation with the PKI).

Political implications

Although the *peranakan* leaders of the assimilationists have consistently denied that they wish to fight Baperki, they cannot escape the implications of their stand. Nor does the fact that many of them come from Catholic, Protestant, and other "right-wing" elements in the Chinese community

---

3   Ong Hok Ham, in *Star Weekly*, 12 September and 3 October 1959. These are two of a series of articles on the Philippines by Ong.

make their arguments that they are free of political motives more convincing.

This political division is clearly evident from the way the Indonesians have reacted to the two sides. While neither Baperki nor the assimilationist group has attracted wide attention or support, both have their promoters in the Indonesian community; Baperki from the "left," the others from the "right."

Baperki supporters, such as Boejoeng Saleh, who has served as Secretary of the Central Committee of Baperki and got his political training in SOBSI, the labor union affiliate of the PKI, are usually hardly typical Indonesians. Lekra, the artists' group which has cooperated with Baperki, is a PKI affiliate. *Harian Rakjat*, the PKI organ itself, has on a number of occasions given support to Baperki's drives.

On the other hand, when the younger proponents of assimilation sought wider support in 1962, they attracted the attention of some members of the military, Colonel Soetjipto of army headquarters and even General Nasution himself. In addition to the army people, a few other Indonesians of the "right" lent their support to the movement's activities in Djakarta. An attempt was made, in 1962, to amalgamate the assimilation forces, under the title Urusan Pembinaan Kesatuan Bangsa (Organization for the Development of National Unity), with the regional Badan Pembina Potensi Karya (Body for the Development of Functional Potentials), a semi-political "front" of businessmen and other interests under military sponsorship.

Certain army leaders are deeply suspicious of the Chinese. This suspicion stems, in part, from a fear of Chinese support for communism or for Communist China's power politics. Nasution is reported to have said that, so long as they remain unassimilated, he regards the Chinese of Indonesia as a potential fifth column. He also remarked in late 1962 that with the settlement of Dutch-Indonesian conflicts over West Irian, the Chinese would find themselves in the position — previously filled by the Dutch — of scapegoat for Indonesia's troubles. These officers naturally welcomed an effort initiated among the Chinese to promote assimilation.

Military support was a two-edged sword for the assimilationists. While it was advantageous to have such powerful backing, one of the motives of these backers was suspicion of the very Chinese they purported to help. Furthermore, the name of the military, instead of lending weight to their cause, tended to inspire the feeling among the Chinese that the assimilationists' suggestions were being forced upon them. Some feared a repetition of earlier anti-Chinese actions which were led by the military. The army had touched off the school closings in 1957-58, it carried out the anti-Kuomintang campaign in 1958, and its role in the alien rural retail and residence bans in 1959-60 hardly helped improve its image among the Chinese.

Views of older and younger generations

After 1962, discussion of assimilation became an emotionally charged matter. Stories circulated among *peranakans* in East Java, for example, that Chinese girls were being accosted with proposals of marriage by Indonesian youths who were strangers to them. "It mustn't be forced," cried the *peranakans* when intermarriage was discussed, as if this were actually what the assimilationists had favored. The older generation of *peranakans*, particularly those who remember vividly the Dutch period, are particularly resistant to the idea of intermarriage. Older *peranakans* expressed fear that a daughter who married an Indonesian might be readily divorced (divorce is relatively common among Moslem Indonesians and rare among Chinese); some of the same parents expressed approval of a daughter's marriage to a European or an American. Polygamy (Islamic law theoretically allows a man to take four wives) is another cause of *peranakan* resistance to intermarriage. But, although polygamy is much discussed, it is not nearly so common among Indonesians as the discussion of it, and it is not unknown for a Chinese man in Indonesia to take a second wife. This opposition to assimilation (especially intermarriage) on the part of the older *peranakans* may be attributed to resistance to Indonesianization among those who can remember the low position held by Indonesians in the colonial society.

If in discussing intermarriage the older generation raises difficulties against it, the young *peranakans* — students and younger graduates — maintain a more open mind on the subject, emphasizing mutual consent, and sometimes, the consent of the parents. Although religious differences remain a barrier, intermarriage is apparently increasing among young *peranakan* Chinese and Indonesians, particularly where both are

Christians. Both young and old recognize that difference of religion compounds the difficulties for a racially mixed marriage. But insofar as the younger generation has had closer association with Indonesians, particularly in the schools, it sees intermarriage as a likely and even desirable proposition, always with the provision, "it must not be forced." Educated Indonesians seem to regard resistance to intermarriage on the part of Chinese as an anachronism. They expect it to occur naturally, except perhaps where religious difference interferes.

The adoption of Indonesian aliases by adult Chinese has given rise to scorn because, in many cases, it is considered as a seeking for preference in business or a display of shame over a person's Chinese ancestry. In some cases, it also gives rise to some good-natured joking, as in the story of the Chinese who asked to take the Indonesian name "Kasno" (from *bekas Tjino*, which literally means ex-Chinese).

On the other hand, more young *peranakan* couples are choosing Indonesian-sounding names, such as Dewi, Arianti, Krishna, for their children, either along with or in place of the Chinese name. In part this replaces an earlier trend (which was not confined to the Christian group) to give Western names to *peranakan* children. Some Indonesians spoke with approval of this trend in child-naming, but their attitude toward an adult's adoption of an Indonesian alias, particularly when his Chinese name was already well known, was less favorable.

That the idea of force has come to be associated with that of assimilation represents a defeat for the movement. It partly resulted from the tactical error of appearing to ally so closely with the military and partly from the success of the Baperki counterattack.

The attention attracted by the fear of forced intermarriage (it must be mentioned again that marriage of Chinese men and Indonesian women has passed without comment for centuries, especially among the lower classes — it is marriage of a Chinese woman to an Indonesian man which arouses resistance) and the discussion of name-changes has detracted from the more basic issues of assimilation: the problem of separate Chinese organizations and institutions in Indonesian society. Understandably, Baperki has contributed to the confusion, for criticism of Chinese societies attacks Baperki itself, together with its affiliated organizations and activities and strikes at the very root of *peranakan* society as it is now organized.

Some *peranakan* organizations have been conscious of this aspect of the problem and have taken various steps to meet it, but almost always within a rather conservative framework. The usual method has been to adopt an Indonesian-sounding translation of its name and to open membership to Indonesians. Thus the *peranakan* religious group Sam Kauw Hui is now Perkumpulan Tribudaja. Some Chinese believers have attempted to stress the Buddhist aspect of their belief in connection with the old Hindu-Buddhist traditions of Java and Bali.[4] The Ta Hsueh Hsueh Sheng Hui, the university students' group now Calls itself Perhimi (*Perhimpunan Mahasiswa Indonesia* — Indonesian Students' Association), and its ordinary members must be Indonesian citizens.[5] One such organization whose Indonesian membership is more than token is a sports club in Palembang, now called Dharma Djaja; over one-third of the members are Indonesians, although a few years ago it was an exclusively Chinese organization.[6]

President Soekarno's intervention

In February 1963, the assimilation-integration controversy reached a climax. The assimilationists attempted to broaden their support by getting President Soekarno's agreement to a statement endorsing their viewpoint. Soekarno told them "A nation with minorities is no nation" and expressed his support for assimilation as an end to "exclusivism."[7]

Up to late 1962, it was questionable whether the vigor of Baperki's attack on assimilation was in proportion to the threat posed by the assimilation movement. The movement never acquired, or even tried to acquire, mass support among the Chinese, particularly after its vehicle *Star Weekly* was closed. But when it did get some support from the both anti-communist and anti-Chinese military, it became particularly dangerous to Baperki. Therefore, Baperki felt it needed the President's support as quickly as possible, since only Soekarno could give an ideological pronouncement

---

4   *Star Weekly*, 30 May and 6 June, 1959.
5   *Republik*, 26 October 1957,
6   Interview, 1962.
7   *Assimilasi dalam rangka pembinaan kesatuan bangsa* (Departemen Penerangan Republik Indonesia, Penerbitan Chusus 259), p. 5.

of sufficient weight to solve this problem. Fortunately for them, the President had previously displayed considerable sympathy for Baperki and its goals.

Some time before his February pronouncement on nation-building and assimilation, Soekarno had been invited to address the Baperki Congress to be held March 14-18, 1963 in Djakarta. In order to demonstrate that they too could rally popular support and thereby encourage Soekarno to take an even stronger pro-assimilation stand, the assimilationists prepared to hold a conference in Djakarta March 10 to 12, just before the opening of the Baperki Congress. In this, they again had military encouragement. An additional motive for the conference was the decision to disband the BPPK in May, when martial law would end, and to dissolve it into the National Front. This meant that previous assimilationist activities under BPPK sponsorship would have to find a new sponsor, and a decision was made at the conference to set up an institute to continue the work.

A number of cabinet ministers and other officials were invited to address the gathering. Most of these did not appear in person but sent written messages, whose tone favored "nation-building" and an end to "sukuism," that is, ethnic exclusivism. One of the most outspoken was Soenario, PNI member, former Foreign Minister and co-signer of the 1955 agreement on dual citizenship. That he even lent his name as adviser to the group throws light on his attitude toward the treaty itself. Soenario argued that the intention of the treaty had been to end the double loyalty of the Indonesian Chinese, so that cultural assimilation to Indonesia should follow rejection of the legal tie of Chinese citizenship. That no reorientation of the cultural values of the citizen Chinese had followed the change in their nominal legal status seemed to him to indicate that the realignment of citizenship had been for nothing. Soenario represents a viewpoint which is widespread among non-communist Indonesian leaders.

The resolutions from this conference struck again at the "exclusive" organizations among the Chinese and even at schools which, although "national" in form were in practice Chinese in student body.[8] These were

---

8   *Ibid.*, p. 50.

clearly directed against Baperki and other successor schools to the old alien schools, and the assimilationists apparently hoped to encourage the government to limit such schools, but they must have recognized that any such government regulation would surely have had adverse effects on many Protestant and Catholic schools, as well as those of Baperki. (Since many supporters of these resolutions came from the Christian group, one is inclined to wonder how much thought they had given to the implementation of their resolution.) Results of the conference were presented to Soekarno for his approval on March 13.

Baperki had begun to rally the support of its left-wing allies against assimilation before its Congress actually opened on March 14. On March 10, *Warta Bhakti* (successor to *Sin Po*, the leading *peranakan* newspaper) published an article by Tan Hwie Kiat, Baperki's information officer, insisting that the only solution to the minority problem must come from the achievement of a just and prosperous society through Indonesian socialism. The following day, *Harian Rakjat* of the PKI presented an editorial on national unity which purported to explain what Soekarno had really meant when he spoke to the assimilationists. "National unity" did not mean that either the Indonesian *sukus* (Buginese, Javanese, Dayak, Batak, etc.) or the groups such as *peranakan* Arabs, Chinese or Indians, would disappear, but only that it would be impossible for them to continue being "cosmopolitan" or "separatist." Forcing people to change their name (*Harian Rakjat* put the emphasis on *force*) would be undemocratic; the important thing was the right to free Indonesia from imperialism and feudalism, from bureaucratic capitalists and landlords.

Siauw opened the Congress on March 14 with an address outlining Baperki's achievements to date, and pointing to the growth of Baperki University and the role which its graduates could play in Indonesian development. He also asked for wider opportunities for Indonesia's one million resident aliens (the great majority of whom are Chinese) to be naturalized as Indonesian citizens.[9] A major portion of the address,

---

9 The naturalization law allows persons born in Indonesia or resident there for five consecutive years (ten non-consecutive years) to acquire Indonesian citizenship if they demonstrate knowledge of Indonesian language and history, pay a fee (scaled to income), and *have no other citizenship* (see Willmott, *op.cit.*, p. 120). To date, very few applicants have actually been naturalized.

however, was concerned with economic problems, including foreign capital and inflation.[10]

If Soekarno's presence at the meeting had not been enough, his keynote address must have given ample satisfaction to Baperki's functionaries. The President not only praised Baperki, urging it to continue to support his programs, but ridiculed the use of the term *asli* ("indigenous") in discussions of Indonesia's minority problem. Indonesia recognized no minority, he asserted, unlike the "socialist countries" with their national minorities. There was no minority, only a number of ethnic groups or *sukus*, including the Chinese *suku* ("*suku Tionghoa*"). The *sukus*, in turn, were so many legs (*kaki*) of the Indonesian body — thus Sundanese, Javanese, Sumatran, Dayak, and *peranakan* Chinese were all parts of the same Indonesian body.[11]

Soekarno probably took this stand in order to avoid alienating either group of the Chinese community, or their respective Indonesian supporters. Baperki has shown itself to have far greater influence among the Chinese themselves, and the President probably felt that his goal, assuring the loyalty and cooperation of the Chinese, could be best met by supporting this group. Nevertheless, Soekarno is interested in national unity. He later encouraged the assimilationists by sponsoring their Institute for the Devel ment of National Unity (*Lembaga Pembinaan Kesatuan Bangsa*) in July 1963. The President, therefore, supported both factions and rejected neither.

1963 riots against Chinese

Although Soekarno was able to say to Baperki that he did not care what kind of a name a person had, so long as he was a patriotic Indonesian, events soon proved that other Indonesians were not so tolerant. In late March 1963, the first of a series of riots against the Chinese occurred in Tjirebon.

The Tjirebon incident was touched off by a court case in which an Indonesian was being tried for the death in August 1962 of a Chinese in a

---

10 Most of the text appeared in *Harian Rakjat*, 15 March 1963.

11 Soekarno, *Baperki supaja mendjadi sumbangan besar terhadap revolusi Indonesia* (Departemen Penerangan Republik Indonesia, Penerbitan Chusus 255).

traffic accident. Both the victim and the accused had been associated with "cross-boy" gangs, and during the course of the trial communal tensions mounted. On March 27, they erupted: Chinese shops were stoned, other Chinese-owned property was damaged or threatened, and order was restored only by the strict imposition of curfews and other controls.

The Tjirebon military commander issued a statement which called for order and, at the same time, cast blame on the Chinese for their ostentatious way of life during a time of economic troubles for the general population. Although there were no further outbreaks in his military district (that is, in the northeast part of West Java), and the commander deserves credit for this, his attitude was not a comfort to the Chinese.

The following May (May 10), an outbreak in Bandung among students of the technical college spread through the city, causing destruction of great amounts of Chinese-owned property, especially motor vehicles and shop inventories. This touched off riots in other cities and towns of West Java: Tegal (actually in western Central Java), Tasikmalaja, Sukabumi, Tjiandjur, Bogor.

While in Bandungj, as in Tjirebon (and probably Tegal), the riots sprang from a single incident, in other towns, such as Sukabumi, which suffered most serious damage, and Tjiandjur, demonstrators arrived in the town by truckloads, and other indications point to deliberate provocation. That the incidents spread in such organized fashion must be attributed to insufficient vigilance on the part of the local military and police. Sukabumi, for instance, is the home of the police academy for all of Java, so it would be difficult to argue that there were insufficient forces to cope with the demonstrators, most of whom were young people. On the other hand, the fact that martial law had only been abolished on May 1 may have contributed to some confusion in the town as to who was responsible for maintaining security. In Djakarta, however, and in towns of Central and East Java such as Semarang and Surabaja, local police prevented any outbreaks by keeping close watch on suspected elements, particularly students. Sympathy incidents also occurred in Medan, Makassar, and Padang.

Almost immediately, on May 13 (May 12 had been a Sunday), the PKI published its denunciation of the incidents, attempting to brand the instigators as economic saboteurs or Masjumi-PSI renegades. The governors of West and Central Java and the national police appealed for order. Although the President had been consulted on means of dealing with the demonstrations, Soekarno's full denunciation came on May 19, after the riots had spread to Sukabumi and Tjiandjur. The major trouble spot was West Java, just as it had been in 1959-60, although in 1963 the authorities did not originate the provocations.

Although the President, the PKI, and subsequently the press tried to lay the blame on dissident right-wing political groups, it appears that economic causes lay at the root of the riots. In Bandung, for example, Chinese were not personally molested by the rioters, and no Chinese lives were lost. Chinese driving cars were made to leave their vehicles; the cars were overturned and set afire, but the owners were not harmed. While the victims offered no resistance which might have provoked the mobs to turn on them, it is nevertheless clear that the rioters were not interested in attacking Chinese so much as Chinese-owned property, to them the symbol of Chinese economic power.

CHAPTER FOUR

INDONESIAN VIEWS OF THE CHINESE

The Baperki view on integration places the burden on the Indonesian majority to accept the Chinese and to banish discrimination. The assimilationists appear to assume that Indonesians will readily accept the Chinese minority, if they will abandon certain of their exclusive habits. Because assimilation has been viewed by some Indonesians and outsiders as a solution to the minority problem, it is worth examining the majority attitude toward the Chinese in more detail, also attempting to explain the causes of the periodic outbreaks against the Chinese.

Cultural pluralism and Indonesian unity

Although the Indonesian motto is "*Bhinneka Tunggal Ika*" ("Unity in Diversity'), even President Soekarno, the nation's number one ideologue, envisages a new all-Indonesian culture in which regional differences will disappear. He recently remarked that Bhinneka (diversity) was "*das Sein*" (what is) and *Tunggal* (unity) "*das Sollen*" (what shall be).[1]

In such a view, assimilation of the citizen Chinese can be only a matter of time and, in fact, most *peranakan* Chinese do foresee an end to Chineseness, but not for some generations. Siauw identifies this with the achievement of a "just and prosperous society."

Even if such a distant utopia is ever realized, for the time being Indonesians must live with cultural pluralism. Although inter-Indonesian ethnic relations occasionally lead to disturbances in some major towns, it is relations between Indonesians and Chinese, the largest

---

1   Assimilasi, *op. cit.*, p. 5.

non-indigenous minority, that give rise to greatest friction and attract most attention.

Despite the fact that the two groups have lived side-by-side for centuries and despite the frequently discussed Indonesian tolerance for differences, time and again Chinese-Indonesian relations have erupted into violence. The incidents marking the campaign against alien retailers in 1959-60 and the outbreaks of March and May 1963 are only the latest of many such instances in the 20th century.

Mass support for anti-Chinese incidents

Any discussion of anti-Chinese incidents or activities, however, must take the distinction between "mass" and "elite" behavior into account.

Frequently it is argued that the Indonesian peasant is not anti-Chinese, and that he even regards the Chinese money-lender as a benefactor (or did in the past when the institution was more prevalent), despite the seemingly outrageous interest rates charged. A *peranakan* Chinese scholar recently wrote of the harmony and mutual tolerance prevailing in a village near Tanggerang,[2] where about one-third of the residents are Chinese *peranakan* farmers, although not far from his research site was the scene of the most famous outbreak against the Chinese in recent times, the Tanggerang incident of May 1946. The argument that the Indonesian masses are tolerant of the Chinese fails to take into account the mass support given to many anti-Chinese incidents.

Sarekat Islam

On the other hand, "elite" attitudes to the Chinese are more easily identified and explained. In the 20th century, the earliest series of anti-Chinese activities centered around the founding of the Sarekat Islam. This organization, the first Islamic-oriented political association, developed from a group formed by Islamic businessmen in 1909 to fight competition from Chinese traders. On the "elite" or leadership level, economic

---

2   Go Gien Tjwan, *Eenheid in verscheidenheid in een Indonesisch dorp* (Dissertation: University of Brussels, 1962).

interest thus reinforced religious resentment in forming attitudes toward the Chinese, who were not only business competitors, but of an alien religion. (This attitude would also be typical of the Masjumi leaders who supported Assaat nearly 50 years later and perhaps also of some West Java leaders.)[3]

The development of Sarekat Islam as a mass movement was marked by anti-Chinese incidents in the ten years after 1909 in a number of Javanese cities, including Solo, Surabaja, and Kudus. In all of these towns, Chinese-Indonesian business competition had been especially keen.[4] The appeal to Islam may here have merely been used to arouse mass opposition to the Chinese. In addition, the Sarekat Islam as an organization must have offered a channel for Indonesians to express real grievances against the Chinese.

Tanggerang incident

In Tanggerang, where the Indonesian revolution brought a particularly cruel attack on the Chinese in May 1946, crude "racial" differences are not the major divisive force between Chinese and Indonesian. In this area in fact Chinese are often physically indistinguishable from Indonesians, and Islam is the most important element dividing the two ethnic groups in the villages. The old Chinese-owned or managed private lands in the area may also have contributed to Indonesian resentment, and several other factors were at work: outside troublemakers, breakdown of authority in a revolutionary situation, economic differences between the two groups, the desire of some youth to display revolutionary zeal. The principal promoters of attacks on the Chinese were irregular armed bands, made up largely of fanatically Islamic groups from Bantam, who had been left in control of the area when the Indonesian army withdrew in May 1946. There is little doubt, however, that the people of Tanggerang also participated in the attacks. An important factor in mobilizing the

---

3 The author is indebted to Professor G. William Skinner, who has emphasized the connection between Islamic parties and anti-Chinese politics in his discussions. For a treatment of the relation of Islam to economic activity, see Clifford Geertz. "Religious Belief and Economic Behavior in a Central Javanese Town," *Economic Development and Cultural Change*, January 1956, esp. pp. 144-152.

4 Willmott, *op. cit.*, p. 12.

masses was almost certainly the appeal of Islam. This is clearly indicated by the fact that, in addition to destroying Chinese life and property, the attackers forced a number of Chinese to be circumcized.[5]

The Indonesian revolution: elite attitudes 1945-49

At the time of the Tanggerang incident the Indonesian government was interested in cultivating Chinese support. In view of the intense pressures on the Republic then, the leaders did their best to uphold Chinese interests. Cooperation with the Chinese consul, for example, was initially good. The citizenship law of 1946[6] recognized all Chinese born in Indonesia as Indonesian citizens, showing a lack of resentment against the Chinese; at the same time it incorporated a provision for Chinese to reject Indonesian citizenship if they wished, something for which the Chinese had fought unsuccessfully in the colonial period. This indicates that the Indonesian elite had a good deal of sympathy for the Chinese at that time, although this in part stemmed from the desire to mobilize Chinese wealth in the Indonesian interest.

Nevertheless, the Republic was unable to do what the Chinese most wanted: guarantee Chinese life and property. It could not control the irregular fighting units on the republican side who were largely responsible for the attacks on property (which were in practice attacks on Chinese). As the revolution wore on, and incidents continued, even some Chinese who were initially sympathetic to the Republic began to feel that only the Dutch forces could or would protect them. Fear of the Indonesians became a moving force for the Chinese, and they formed their own self-defense organization, the Pao An Tui. It, therefore, appeared to the Indonesians that the Chinese were fighting alongside the Dutch, The mutual mistrust between Chinese and Indonesians engendered during

---

5   Rosihan Anwar published a series of articles defending the position of the Indonesian Republic in Merdeka in June 1946. *Star Weekly* and *Sin Po* (the latter even more outspoken) give the Chinese side. Go, *op. cit.*, pp. 149 and 218, emphasizes that no incidents took place in the village he studies because no outsiders had stirred up trouble. According to other sources, Dutch forces had been in control of the area around his village, east of the town of Tanggerang, and were able to maintain order. The Tanggerang incidents all took place in the vacuum between the advancing Dutch forces and the retreating Indonesian army, an area left in the control of irregular, undisciplined bands.
6   Part of the law is in Willmott, *op. cit.*, pp. 113-114. The full text is reprinted in Baperki, *Segala sesuatu tentang kewarganegaraan Republik Indonesia* (Djakarta: Baperki, n. d.), pp. 75-82.

the revolution persists to this day and has greatly influenced Indonesian elite attitudes toward the Chinese.

Elite attitudes 1950-57: Islamic parties

The attitude of the Indonesian elite toward the Chinese from 1950 to 1957 can be discussed in terms of the political parties. In dealing with the Chinese, the parties were not acting in response to mass pressures, but in the context of their own ideas or of some chance for political gain.

The most important Islamic party, Masjumi, when in control of the Natsir cabinet, introduced policies favoring *asli* (indigenous) Indonesian businessmen over Chinese.[7] The arrests under its successor, the Sukiman cabinet (again Masjumi) in August 1951 were both anti-Communist and anti-Chinese (not only were many PKI leaders imprisoned, but some non-Communist Chinese were arrested as well), representing a further coalescence of basic attitudes.

After 1952, the Masjumi split into the modernist Masjumi and conservative Islamic Nahdatul Ulama. While the new Masjumi was the more active and more anti-Communist, both continued the attitudes of the parent party toward the Chinese. Thus, in 1956, when its political fortunes were ebbing, the Masjumi espoused the Assaat movement, a vigorous attack on the Chinese position in the economy, probably in the hopes of regaining some popular support. Although the NU was perhaps more discreet in the matter, its sympathies were with Assaat as well. When the Masjumi was virtually out of the political picture, in May 1959, an NU member, Minister of Trade Rachmat Muljomiseno, formulated the attack on alien retailers.

The Indonesian attitude towards the Chinese is not simply a matter of religious difference, however. If Indonesia is the world's largest Islamic nation, it is probably also the most tolerant (perhaps syncretistic is a better word). The religious difference between Chinese and Indonesian, although important, does not exist in isolation. Like the early Sarekat Islam, the Moslem parties in Indonesia have derived a great deal of their

---

7 See Amstutz, *op. cit.*, for a fuller discussion of the government policies toward Indonesian businessmen.

support from a class of traders (in Java) whose devotion to business has matched their devotion to religious goals. For the Masjumi, this support came more from the Outer Islands; for the NU, from Java. This economic base among the traders helps explain why the anti-Chinese activity of both these parties most often took the form of government decisions to restrict the Chinese place in the economy by reserving favors for Indonesian businessmen.

The nationalists, 1950-57

Different motives prompted the secular nationalists, the PNI and others like them, but their policies were anti-Chinese nonetheless. Although the first Ali Sastroamidjojo (PNI) cabinet (July 1953-July 1955) had two ministers of Chinese descent, it vigorously implemented policies in favor of indigenous businessmen. In part, the PNI may have been feathering its own nest, with an eye to the need for funds in the 1955 elections. In part, the nationalists were motivated by the conviction that it was unjust and even dangerous to have so much of the country's wealth and trade controlled by alien hands. By "alien" they often meant citizen Chinese as well. These nationalists, whose attitude is shared to a greater or less degree by many educated Indonesians, especially in Java, believe that even citizen Chinese businessmen cannot be trusted to do business in the best interests of Indonesia because of their family and business ties abroad. That this argument is largely based on prejudice can be inferred from the fact that it fails to distinguish between *totok* and *peranakan*. Any severe disruption in the Indonesian economy, as at the time of PP-10, becomes, for the nationalist, a proof of the perniciousness of the Chinese role in the Indonesian economy. He ignores the fact that the disruption was precipitated by the severity of the Indonesian attack on Chinese trade. Chinese shopkeepers faced with the prospect of imminent confiscation of their source of livelihood could hardly be expected to continue business as usual.

The nationalists, arguing that Indonesia can never be really free while its economy is so much at the mercy of aliens and those of alien descent, consider the predominant economic position of the Chinese to be a result of conscious Dutch policy to weaken and control the Indonesians. This attitude, although it has a little historical basis, is often exaggerated and distorted. To many Indonesians, the Chinese personify the evils of the colonial system as much as do the Dutch.

Indonesian nationalists also resent that most *peranakan* Chinese are uninterested in Indonesian politics and attribute this to favoritism for the Dutch or for China. In recent years, any city-dwelling Indonesian could observe the enthusiasm displayed by *totok* Chinese for Chinese national days or the public celebration of Chinese religious festivals. The *peranakan* Chinese apathy and distaste for Indonesian political activities then appear to some nationalists as caused by lack of loyalty to Indonesia.

The fact that a substantial proportion of the *peranakans* have had Dutch education and that many continue to speak Dutch to their children is another irritant. (Older Indonesians of the elite may converse in Dutch, but it is dying out quickly and the young seldom learn more than a few words.) In short, in addition to the problem of Chinese cultural difference, Western influence among the *peranakans* (particularly in the years of bad relations with the Dutch) has irritated Indonesian observers.

In the Moslem view, a solution to the minority problem can only come with conversion of the Chinese to Islam, There is evidence that Chinese Moslems have been assimilated as Indonesians, but this happened either before the European period or only in isolated areas. At present, Chinese who are converted to Islam are often suspected by both sides, and conversion is not a popular solution. The nationalist opinion admits the possibility of assimilation Thus if a Chinese accepts Indonesian citizenship, abandons the public display of Chinese (or *peranakan*) culture for Indonesianization, associates in organizations (including business and politics) with Indonesians, and enters as fully as possible into Indonesian society, he can be accepted. There is today considerable evidence that Chinese who meet Indonesians at the same socio-economic level pass rather quickly into Indonesian society: Chinese *peranakan* students, government employees, and even in some areas, businessmen have testified to this.

Essentially, the secular nationalist asks that the Chinese "overcompensate," giving clear proof of their loyalty to Indonesia, before they may be fully accepted as Indonesians. This was an element in the Indonesian approach to the dual citizenship treaty (which was signed by a PNI cabinet), a feeling that if the citizen Chinese were forced to go through a court declaration of their loyalty to Indonesia, they would somehow be more devoted to Indonesian politics and culture.

But "overcompensation" or any steps toward assimilation must have a positive motivation. So far Indonesian government citizenship policies, alien taxes, and other forms of discrimination have contributed to making the citizenship choice a purely self-interested one. *Peranakan* Chinese without hesitation have ascribed the dual citizenship choice to self-interested calculation. Because the problem of economic discrimination looms so large, many steps toward formal assimilation, such as adopting an Indonesian name or the Islamic religion, are suspected by both Chinese and Indonesians.

The PKI, 1950-63

Of all the major parties, only the PKI has unequivocally supported acceptance of the Chinese *peranakans* as they are. The PKI has protested nearly every inconvenience visited on the Chinese, from the dual citizenship treaty's active system to the alien tax. It even defended the Chinese at the time of the alien retail ban in 1959-60, a position which was highly unpopular at the time (although in retrospect, the PKI does not seem to have suffered much from its stand). *Harian Rakjat* argued that nationalization of big European businesses should precede attacks on the retail shops of poor Chinese.[8]

Observers have viewed this pro-Chinese stance either as subservience to the Chinese Embassy or as a defense of Chinese who might be contributing towards the PKI coffers. In many cases, the PKP's support of the Chinese has really been an attack on its own enemies. This is particularly evident in the abuse heaped on the Assaat movement by the PKI where *Harian Rakjat's* attack on Assaatism was as much an assault on the Masjumi as a defense of the Chinese. Doubtless the PKI feared that its opposition had seized on an extremely popular issue and attacked it accordingly.

In an important case where Chinese interests conflicted with PKI political interests, the PKI indicated that defending the Chinese was of

---

8   *Harian Rakjat*, 23 November 1959 to 8 December 1959.

secondary importance. In late 1953, the Ali cabinet revised the regulations governing importers in a manner which proved to be highly unfavorable to Chinese businessmen. In November of that year Parliament discussed these policies, following an interpellation of a Masjumi member. Siauw took an active part in the discussions, using his speech to evaluate Indonesia's policies for building a "national economy" and to urge the new cabinet not to indulge in *asli* politics. He urged that the government consider carefully the bad effects which favoritism of *aslis* would have on the Indonesian society and economy. Siauw did not, however, specifically attack the policies of the cabinet then in office.

One of the PKI representatives in Parliament also spoke on this point; Sakirman made some criticism of policies which had been carried out by the previous "Masjumi-PSI regime" which, he said, had favored only importers who were Masjumi-PSI party members. On behalf of the PKI, however, he expressed full confidence in the cabinet's plans to work for a national economy. Although the steps the cabinet was taking at the time were not perfect, in general he considered them to be forthright and bold. Among the other actions he praised was the cabinet's decision to send a trade mission to the People's Republic of China.[9]

In this case, the PKI was supporting a cabinet which was initiating measures harmful to Chinese business; in fact, the Ali cabinet took office with PKI support in Parliament. The PKI was not prepared to trade its political advantage merely for the sake of defending the Chinese.

As late as 1963, the PKI's attitude on the assimilation question was also influenced by domestic political considerations, for certain military personnel who were extremely unsympathetic to the PKI were on the side of the assimilationists. The PKI is, therefore, most pro-Chinese when those who are anti-Chinese are anti-Communists. The risk in such a policy is probably less that the party will lose popular supporters (this obviously has not happened to date) than that at a time like 1959-60 it might provoke the military to retaliate against it by a too-vigorous defense of the Chinese. *Harian Rakjat* was closed in December 1959 for defending the Chinese.

---

9 *Ichtisar Parlemen* (Djakarta: Kementerian Penerangan, 1953), No. 197, p. 1118; No. 198, p. 1119 and 1120-1121. Siauw was already a member of Parliament in November 1953, although Baperki was not founded until 1954.

In May 1963, the PKI tried to blame the discredited Masjumi-PSI elements and rebels for the anti-Chinese riots. The party also pointed out that the riots were directed against Soekarno and that they attacked the whole people by destroying supplies of food and other basic necessities. In this case, it encouraged its members to cooperate with the police and military in restoring order.[10]

Baperki finds allies in PKI, Partindo

Despite its defense of the Chinese, the PKI would be embarrassed if large numbers of Chinese flocked to join the party. This may account in part for Tan Ling Djie's minor role in the PKI over the past ten years, although his initial fall from power resulted from a disagreement with the present party leader, Aidit, over party policies. Today, *peranakan* Chinese interested in politics, especially left-wing politics, gravitate instead to Baperki. The frequent cooperation between Baperki leadership and the PKI thus provides a way for the PKI to maintain links with sympathetic Chinese without having the embarrassment of a number of Chinese in its own leadership.

In 1963, perhaps in order to refute the charges of alliance with the PKI, Baperki seemed to be seeking closer ties with a relatively new, left-wing nationalist party, Partindo. Three of Baperki's 1963 board of officers were also active in Partindo leadership, H. Winoto Danuasmoro, Oei Tjoe Tat, and Phoa Thwan Hian.[11] Partindo is by definition a nationalist party, devoted to full adherence to all of Soekarno's ideology. Because of its reputedly close relations with Soekarno, its influence is greater than its mass base. By 1963 the party was considered to be strongly PKI-infiltrated.

Baperki leaders themselves justify their left-wing policies, particularly the informal Partindo alliance, as an attempt to draw near to Soekarno for his protection. But this has never brought them into conflict with the PKI, which is presently working very hard to do just the same thing. For many of Baperki's supporters, of course, discussion of Baperki-PKI

---

10 *Harian Rakjat*, 13-20 May 1963.
11 *Warta Bhakti*, 20 March 1963 and interview, 1963.

relations is irrelevant. To them, the important thing is that the PKI has never sponsored nor obviously condoned discrimination against the Chinese. In need of allies to protect their interests, Indonesia's Chinese will find them where they can.

The *peranakan* Chinese as a whole have never paid much attention to ideology. It could be argued that this alliance with the PKI represents the same kind of "opportunism" which caused many Chinese to appear to ally with the Dutch during the Indonesian revolution; in both cases, their actions were motivated by the need for protection rather than by positive support for the group concerned.

Conceivably, Baperki, in allying itself with the PKI and also seeking Soekarno's protection, hoped to forestall any further elite-level attacks on the Chinese, However, in view of the important role now played by the third and strongest element of the elite, the army, in Indonesian public life, and of the army's unsympathetic attitude to the Chinese, these hopes are not likely to be realized. Baperki's relations with the PKI and the left-wing of Indonesian politics may instead merely serve to increase the army's distrust of the Chinese.

Furthermore, by perpetuating what can almost be called a traditional Chinese community organization and encouraging the Chinese to believe that they can be accepted in Indonesia on their own social and cultural terms, Baperki may be performing a disservice to its constituents which is not offset by the good it has done for them.

Importance of economic problems

Baperki has rightly argued that an ultimate solution to the minority question will come only with great social change. One might add, "great economic change" as well, for economic problems have lain at the base of much Indonesian resentment of the Chinese. One example of the way in which present economic conditions have contributed to bad Chinese-Indonesian relations in the cities, at least, is the effect of inflation.

The last few years have witnessed a spiral of rising prices, one sign of the disruption of the Indonesian economy. Like any inflationary process, it has fallen with different effect on the different sectors of the economy. Self-sufficiency has been a boon to many farmers, and some who have watched this trend have argued that they are relatively better off as a result of higher prices for their produce.

In the cities, however, a sharp contrast is evident between the effect of inflation on the white-collar salaried class and on the business class. The former — government employees, teachers, and others — have been forced to meet rising costs on totally inadequate salaries by taking on two or more supplementary jobs, cashing in on savings (either money or goods), and relying on the government's periodic sales of low-priced rice and other necessities. A trader, businessman, or professional person can escape the effects of rising costs by raising the prices he charges. This is not to argue that businessmen have not felt the effects of economic disruption, certainly most of them must work harder even to stay at the level they maintained a few years ago. But the effects of inflation on the two groups nevertheless do contrast sharply.

In Indonesian towns today, Indonesians tend to work for salaries — even those employed in businesses are most frequently in government businesses and therefore on quite low, fixed salaries. Chinese tend to be private businessmen. The dichotomy is not perfectly rigid, of course; more *totok* Chinese are in business, many *peranakans* work for salary. Nevertheless, this division has led many politically articulate Indonesians to believe that the Chinese are profiting from the present situation while the Indonesians become increasingly worse off. Small wonder, then, that the most recent anti-Chinese activities (Spring 1963) were attacks by urban youth on Chinese properties.

Even should the Indonesian authorities refrain from undertaking policies detrimental to Chinese interests, economic difficulties may of themselves foster resentment against the Chinese. In such a situation, further incidents could result from relatively little provocation. So long as the deterioration of Indonesia's economy persists, prospects for better Chinese-Indonesian relations are anything but encouraging.

INDEX

This book is indexed using Google Book Search at books.google.com.